THE
TEMIARS
OF THE
PUYAN RIVER

HISTORY, CULTURE AND SITUATION
OF THE ORANG ASLI OF POS GOB

VOL. **2**

BY

DAVID P. QUINTON

SUPPORTED BY

  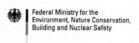

PUBLISHER

ISBN: 978-1-7391344-4-0
Hardback edition.

Layout by Tong Kar Yew, Mediarc Communications
Cover art, Illustrator: Mun Kao, Colourist: Tan Vei Xhane

CONTENTS

Chapter 8

Chapter 9

Chapter 10

Chapter 11

List of Tables

List of Maps and Figures

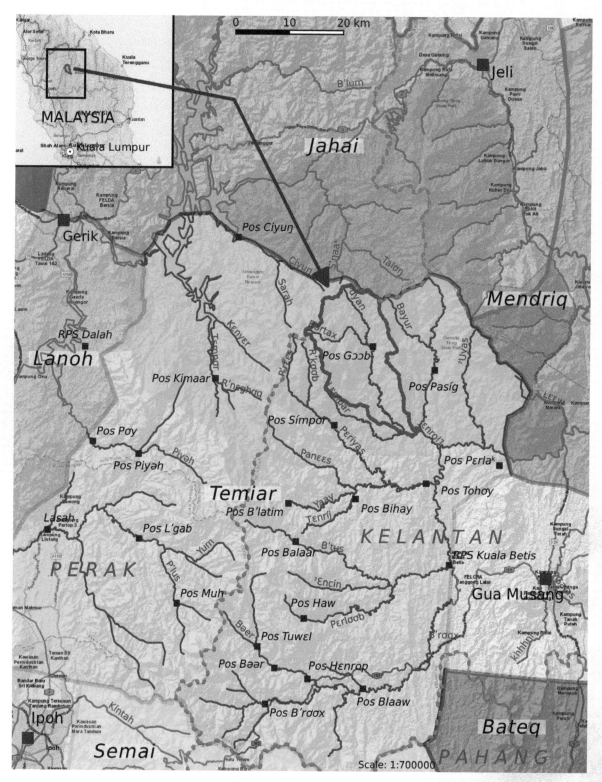

Fig. 1. Map showing the location of Pos Gɔɔb and its river territory, in western Kelantan, Malaysia.

INTRODUCTION

Whereas in Volume 1, containing Chapters 1 through 4, I describe the traditions, beliefs and lifestyle of the Puyan Temiars (especially pre-1950s), in this second volume, containing Chapters 5 through 11, I give a record of their origins and ancestry, and an account of their recent history, from the time of the Emergency until present. Piecing the facts together has taken much time, due to the fact that the Temiars themselves have no notes of their history, it is all held in their memory. Had I been with them during the times of the relocation and the return to their homeland, or even way before that, in the peaceable days when contact with the outside was minimal, I would surely know much more about their ancestors and would be able to expand on the history with many stories. But perhaps these stories will still be found out yet.

Chapter 5, a catalog of herbal medicines known to the Temiars, demonstrates how rich their knowledge of the natural environment is, such knowledge that is still mostly unknown to the outside world and subsequently often under-valued. In Chapter 6, the Temiar concept of land ownership is explained, as being inherited by each kin group from their ancestors, who first settled in the river valleys, roamed the mountains and named every place to leave a heritage to their descendants.

In Appendix 2, a list of 1000 geographic place names in the Puyan Valley is given, demonstrating how bonded the Temiars are to the land and how they are ruly native, as all these names are derived from their knowledge of species, the dreams and experiences of their ancestors and their language.

The Preface in Volume 1 describes in detail how I commenced on this project and began writing the story of the Temiars. There is also a guide to spelling (Vol. 1, xxvii) to aid the reader with pronunciation of Temiar.

Markings on a Temiar blowpipe.

Cadag

Bɛrdaax

Pɛnluᵏ Go'b

Laŋɛɛd

Kasay

To the Temiars, the forest is full of plant species that can be used as natural remedies.

5 | HERBAL MEDICINES OF THE TEMIARS

Herbal medicines played an important role in the Temiars' every day life and their knowledge of plants, vines and roots which could be applied to cure illness was very comprehensive indeed. To date, I have listed close to a hundred plants with their uses and this list could probably double, with more time to research them. A day's walk with the Temiars of Píɲcɔʻɔŋ village and I discover a dozen or more plant species, that are frequently collected by the Temiars or are known for their efficacy. Common problems that natural remedies would be sought for include stomach ache, fever, high temperature, colds, rashes, scabies, cuts and burns, muscle and joint pains, dizziness, blacking out, breathlessness and conditions caused by tabooed animals.

This chapter does not aim to be a complete or thorough survey of Temiar knowledge in this area, as to do that might take me another ten years! I hope, however, that it will be something of an identification help, and, in the least, a good introduction to Temiar medicinal practice.

Tadəəd

Tadəəd root

The use of herbal remedies among the Temiars comes completely second nature to them. As soon as an illness is heard of, or the chances arise that someone might get sick, suggestions will be made of the plants or vines that should be sourced, to treat and alleviate the health problem. A sick person would not collect herbs themselves, however, as, if they did, the remedies would lose efficacy, but others

A herbal tea prepared from tadəəd root, for curing stomach ache.

would need to gather them instead. When the sick were children, the father, grandfather or other relative would disappear into the forest to gather the specific herbs which they knew would help. Temiars with an eye for plants would spot specific herbs while gathering materials, such as rattan, for example, or while hunting frogs at the river, and would make a note of where they had seen them. In this way they could return later to the right place, whenever they needed to gather them.

Medicinal herbs which could grow easily (especially those from the zingiber family of plants) would be planted around the home, so that they could be gathered and applied quickly, as needs arose. Those who might not succeed at locating them in the forest could also make use of them more easily, if they were found nearby. A grandmother, for example, would dig some *moŋlɛɛy* root tubers, and grate them to make a herbal bath for a sick family member, or some *r'tam* root to make a chalky wash for a grandchild with a high temperature. Those who were spiritual would *p'taa*[k], or recite over (Malay, jampi), and *t'hool*, or blow, on the herbs, calling on their dream guide, or a revealed form of Nyʉ[k] ²Alʉj, in order for them to produce the best results.

In the old days, when a Temiar became ill, he or she would walk deep into the forest and stay there a while, with a companion, or their family, finding whatever herbs they could to revive their health. Today, the Temiars still take off into the forest, on occasions, when they feel they need to return to nature and escape the pollutants that, to them, are attached to modern living—the forest is their free health spa! It is their place of tranquility where they immerse themselves to find mental and physical well-being.

Pasùg

G'wòòm

G'lapoh

Panúl

R'mɛɛd root

R'mɛɛd

Grated r'mɛɛd

I begin my list, here, with cures for the stomach, seeing that stomachache and diarrhea are possibly the most common health problems, due to unseen contaminants in food and water that are often consumed. It was also a remedy for the stomach that gave me my first positive experience with their herbal medicine. We were camping up at the Kacəŋ River, and I had a sudden bout of diarrhea (which they said was due to exposure to the cool air at the waterfall we stopped to photograph) and one of the group went quickly to find a special root for me. That root was from the *tadəəd* tree, and they boiled it and I drank its tea, which was hot in the throat, and the problem was instantly settled. I also recently made this tea myself, without any stomach complaints at the time, and it made me drowsy and it felt like it detoxed my gut.

In case there was no *tadəəd* tree around, several other herbs could also be used as treatments for gastric pain and diarrhea. The *kadɔɔᵏ-daax, pasùg* and *g'woóm* vines could be used in the same way as *tadəəd,* boiled as a herbal tea. The *g'lapoh* tree was another cure, the bark of which was boiled. The leaves of *paɲííl,* a flowering plant growing at cool rivers, were cooked and eaten to settle a sore stomach. The *kolím* nut (pictured, Vol. 1, p117) was chewed raw as a cure for stomach problems, and its bitter, hot properties were able to deal with intestinal worms also. *R'mɛɛd,* the turmeric root (*Curcuma longa*), was a vital herb, and was used as a remedy for *r'waac,* or prolonged or bloody diarrhea. It was grated and mixed in water to make into a drink. Its strong, yellow colour was also valued and they would cook it with snail shells in a bamboo tube, to make a dye for their basket and pouch weaving.

One of the most important plants used by the Temiars for its medicinal properties, was the *pɛnyaaw*, or spiral ginger (*Costus speciosus*), else known by them as *laŋɛɛd maŋsiiᵏ*, a soft cane which can grow twenty feet high. For medicinal purpose, it was made into a *tɛmpuŋ*, beaten into fibers, so that its water could be squeezed on someone with fever, and given them to drink, and the fibers were wrapped around their forehead. The plant is known to herbalists from Africa and India, to Papua, and the Temiars claim that it can even cure malaria.[1] It is called *maŋsiiᵏ*, today, by ritual dance practitioners among the Temiars, who hang it at the centre of the dance hall, and bathe their heads with its cooling water after a dance. The variety with a hairy stem is known to be poisonous, however.

Pɛnyaaw: a spiral ginger commonly used by Temiars for treating fever; the canes flourish in wet areas.

When Temiars, young and old alike, felt *jiiᵏ*, or ill, and had a *bʉd ʔulah*, or high temperature, certain plants that produced a cooling effect on the body would be sourced to help reduce their fever. There were over a dozen such plants, known for their cooling properties, with the *pɛnyaaw* cane being the most vital of these but the *c'moɓg* vine was also sourced for the cooling water it contained. The stem of *ʔapoɓs ləwɛɛy*, a tall zingiber plant, was cut and beaten and added to water. *Tiʔux*, the fresh water contained in live bamboo, was drunk to reduce a fever, and also *toɓx*, the 'chalk' found inside the base of a bamboo cavity, when the bamboo contains water, also had a cooling effect and was smeared on the forehead. Another cure for fever was the *l'muuŋ* plant, a large limpet, the fruits of which, resembling bananas, were eaten.

With other plants, the leaves would be soaked in water for a few hours and then the water would be used to bathe with. They included *galox, hənaroox, ʔancōōᵏ, morɛɛt, lɛmpux, jaram, jɛrnaŋ, cɛlcoɓl, mənyap* vine, *k'boɓx, lɛriyaar* and *cɛdroɓd pantɛy*. Even the *carax* flower (*Celosia argentea spicata*, pictured, Vol. 1, p47) and *riyɛɛs lalaŋ*, or elephant grass roots, could be used to cool a fever. Many Temiars might refer to these as *ʔubad sɛdŋɛɛ̄d*, or child medicines, due to the fact that it is primarily children who raise the most concern when they become feverish and people *gadís*, or hurry, to gather these herbs for them.

5.1 Before making a journey into another river valley or unknown area, a whole flask-full of this cane water would be squeezed out and the whole family would drink it, to ensure safety from malaria during their time away.

C'moɡ

Ləwɛɛy flower

ˀApoˀos ləwɛɛy

Toˀox

Toˀox, the white residue found inside bamboo was collected and smeared on the face. to cool high temperature.

L'mʉʉɲ

Galox

Hənaroox

ʔAncōōᵏ

Lɛmpux

Mɔʹrɛɛt

Jaram

Jɛrnaŋ

Lɛriyaar

Cɛlcoʾol

Tali^k mənyap

K'boʾx

Cɛdroʾoʾd pantɛy

Another important remedy was made with the white root of the home *r'tam* plant (which is smaller than the forest variety). To prepare it, the root was first grated into pulp and mixed in water, and then left for half an hour to settle, producing a solid residue of the plant's starch. The yellowish water was then poured off and the white starch was mixed with fresh water to make a milky suspension, which could be drunk and bathed with. The results were a cooling of the body and also soothing of a sore throat.

Stages of r'tam starch preparation: 1. grated pulp mixed in water, 2. strained and left to settle, 3. the solid is mixed with fresh water.

Persons believed to be suffering with *sabat* illness, caused by a breach of a game taboo, whether of their own doing or of their parents' while they were still in the womb, were prone to having seizures and having burning hot temperatures. Usually, they were children, but adults also could suffer from it. Certain plants were sourced to bathe them with, such as *taroʹg* and *soʹog boʹt*, but only knowledgeable people would be able to find them. They would also need to have continual treatments in order for any improvement to occur.

Taroʹg

Soʹog boʹt

When a person *caaᵏ sùᵏwad*, or caught a cold, and had nasal congestion with a sore throat, a different category of plants would be sourced to give them relief. The *pɛnyaaw* cane water was not given in this case and it was deemed dangerous as it could exasperate the condition, causing a person breathing difficulty. One cure was the leaf of a montane tree, called *s'dùx*, which smells like Sarsi (a popular Malaysian soft drink), but this was not found in the lowland. Another cure was *boʹod bɛmhup*, or 'fart leaf', which has an unpleasant odour, and this was found throughout the forest. Another was the new shoot of *bahoʹoᵏ*, also called *p'rɛnhɛg*, a fragrant zingiber, which was hot to the taste and was chewed whenever a person felt a sore nose or throat. Its flower was also picked if available and squeezed in water to make a drink. The root of the *bayuur* tree was also scraped and soaked to make a medicine for colds, as was *tɛnruul* root (mentioned below).

The small buttress of the bayuur tree was cut and split open to make a knife sheath. Its roots were also used as a herbal medicine.

Baho'o*k*

Bo'o'd bɛmhup

Baho'o*k* flower

S'dux

Certain plants were so effective for maintaining health they were always planted around the house, to make them available when needs arose, and especially for administering fast remedies to their children. These included *moŋlɛɛy, kayaaᵏ, ʔuloˊx* and *cadag*, all zingiber species, as well as *r'mɛɛd, bɛrdaax* and *r'tam*, of the Curcuma genus, and *tabaar*, a spiral ginger. The preparation of these plants was simple and it took only minutes to make a bath or drink with which to treat a sick person. The plant's tubers were dug up and washed, grated on a thorn stick (the same method as with yams and *soˊic* nuts), and then mixed with water and strained, to produce an instant juice of the plant. With *cadag*, or beehive ginger (*Zingiber spectibile*), its spectacular, yellow and red flowers were crushed and mixed in water, and a person who felt ill could also bathe with the rain water that had collected in the flower's 'cups'.

The two zingiber plants used in cooking, *j'maad* and *moˊoŋ* (pictured, Vol. 1, p116), were also valuable for treating illness, their roots being smashed to make juice to bathe with and their stems flattened and tied around the forehead. Yet another zingiber plant, *lɛmpoˊoj*, a soft-leafed variety found only at high altitudes, was used in the same way, to relieve a headache (thought to be more effective than *kɛnwoˊox*, mentioned below) and was also used for bringing down a high temperature.

Cadag

Cadag

Lɛmpoˊoj

There was probably not a single zingiber plant, known to the Temiars, that didn't have a beneficial use, health-wise, with a dozen varieties used in herbal medicine, and the rest providing sweet, zesty fruits and also culinary flavoring. In the old days, before the arrival of sugar and artificially sweetened things, the Temiars would forage the zingiber fruits in their season, such as *ʔapoʻoʻs boʻt* (left), that tastes of tangerine, collecting them by the basket-load. Then they would extract and mash the fruits in bamboo, and drink the pure nectar from the tube. (More fruiting varieties are pictured in Vol. 1, p91.)

The two plants *bɛrdaax* (*Curcuma euchroma*) and *moŋlɛɛy* (sometimes called *moŋlaay*), played an important role in health protection and they would be the first thing prepared for a person who was *tɛdhaat*, or lain down and unable to rise. With the latter plant, the water of which looks and tastes like orange juice, a little would be drunk by the sick person and then the rest bathed with, whereas with *bɛrdaax*, the water was only bathed with. The pulp left over after straining the water from the grated root was used to *subəəy*, or scatter around the home, to cleanse it from anything causing the illness. Villagers were also aware that visiting places far away, or people coming back from downriver, and these days, from town, could bring with them *cʼnɛɛᵏ*, or something detrimental to everyone's health, so these kind of remedies provided them with a wall of protection. A person going off on a journey or heading downriver would also bathe with the herbal water to make themselves untouchable by illness, and even magic spells, while away.

Moŋlɛɛy

Moŋlɛɛy root

ʔAsuh ʔAti, of Píncɔˀɔŋ village, grates moŋlɛɛy root on a thorn stick, to make a bathing juice.

Bɛrdaax

Bɛrdaax flower

Bɛrdaax root

When a person felt *loyɛc*, or dizzy, and they had trouble standing, they could be treated with the root of *ʔulóx*, the juice of which was extracted by pounding and was applied to the forehead (it was also used for painting the face yellow). Likewise, the root of *kayaaᵏ* could be applied in the same way, to cure dizziness, but it was also a cure for extreme stomach pain, if a person could bare to drink it, due to its very hot taste. They would also give it to a dog to make its mouth burn hot, so that it would bark at animals, and become a tracking hound.

A *tɛŋóʾr kuuy*, or migraine, which often accompanied fever or flu, would be treated with certain herbs to give relief. *Kɛŋwóʾox*, a forest zingiber that was easily identified by the dark stripes on its leaves, would be cut and its stem flattened and worn around the forehead as a headband. The leaves of the *tabaar* plant were pressed on the forehead to treat migraines and fever. Another was the *bɛjsíj* plant, which produces yellow fruits with prickly hairs (pictured, Vol. 1, p123), the leaves of which were lain near the fire to blanch them and then pressed on the forehead.

ʔUlóx root

Planted kayaaᵏ

Samsudin B'kəd holds a wild kayaaᵏ plant, a fragrant zingiber with a hot-tasting root.

Kɛŋwoʾox

Tabaar

A headband made of kɛŋwoʾox stem is worn, for alleviating a migraine.

Bəər l'haaw, the new shoots of a small tree, was cooked and eaten by older people, to make them feel vigorous in body, so that they could get up and go easily, and walk far without feeling tired. The leaves of the *g'rōᵏ* tree were boiled to make a tea, which a person would drink when feeling off colour, in the evening, so that they would wake up in the morning feeling well. Another herbal tea was made from the root of the *cihuŋ* tree, which was found only at high altitudes. It was highly valued by Temiars in the old days and they would collect it whenever they wandered on the mountains. It was said that whoever drank it frequently would never be touched by illness.

The *tɛmtɔɔp* vine, a leathery vine root found hanging from trees at the river, was braided into waist bands and head bands, to be worn for promoting good health. The latter was called *tɛmpɔɔᵏ ʾAlʉj*, headband of ʾAlʉj, as it was thought to give health directly from the Creator.

Cihuŋ

Bəər l'haaw

G'rơ^k

Belts and a headband made of braided
tɛmtɔɔp vine.

Jarɨ́j

The soft jarɨ́j leaf was used to
clean dirt from the face.

Cuts and burns were common to the Temiars who lived in an environment of sharp natural materials, such as split bamboo, and today's bush knife, and who always gathered around an open fire, with water boiling in spilling bamboo tubes. For cuts, the *bɔrcaap* fern and *cɔɔg mamoʔᵏ*, the wild banana flower, were used as antiseptics. To stop bleeding, *seŋkoʔoʔᵏ ʔawɛn*, the scrapings of green bamboo skin was applied to a cut, and also *ʔakoʔw*, dried tobacco leaf, was applied to deep cuts and tied on with a band, to allow them to heal quickly. For burns and scalds, the stem of the *cadít* plant was scraped and then rubbed together between the hands to create a lather, which was applied to the wound.

Cɛgloʔg and *cɛdroʔoʔd* leaves were both used to treat cuts so that they would heal fast, but they also had other uses besides. *Cɛgloʔg* was also used to treat general illness, while *cɛdroʔoʔd* was used to treat inflammation and joint pain.

Slaaᵏ bɔrcaap

Cadít

Mamoʔᵏ

Cɛgloʔg

Cɛdroʔoʔd

Even the weeds in the bushes around the house found a place in the Temiars' herbal medicine. The *balùd* leaf, a small creeper, could be used as an antiseptic for cuts. A large amount was picked and rubbed between the hands until it produced a juice, which was then squeezed onto a wound. *Taŋhoy*, a fast-growing plant that takes over any clear space in a couple of months, was heated over the fire and applied to sprains, and it was also boiled and eaten to help settle a stomachache. *B'rɛlnyoʻol*, another small plant, was also used for treating sprains.

Taŋhoy

B'rɛlnyoʻol

Balùd

'Akoʻw

Herbal remedies prepared for post-natal mothers and their new-born children were highly important to the Temiars and would be prepared as soon as the mother was noticed to be in labour or had given birth (as many mothers preferred to give birth alone, without any fuss). These included *pɛnlu^k goʾb*, for reducing pain, and *kacip*, a ground-creeping vine, to heal the womb, both of which were made into tea and were drunk by the mother.[2] The bud of the *manaar* vine, or rafflesia, was once used as a post-natal remedy but it was found to be too potent (being a tabooed *julux* species) and it caused women to *sɛdsiid*, or become deranged. Two herbs used for rubbing on the abdomen of a mother after childbirth were *j'waaŋ* and *bəər k'laab*, an edible plant (pictured, Vol. 1, p116). *Buŋaa^k rayə*, the hibiscus flower, was pounded and mixed in water, and was drunk by expectant mothers, to enable them to give birth easily.

Kacip

Rayə

Pɛnlu^k goʾb

5.2 The day after giving birth, the mother would sit on a heap of hot sand overed with plant leaves (such as, *taŋhoʾy, cɛlcoʾol* and *p'rɛnhɛg*) which were stuffed in a bamboo tube and steamed beforehand, to aid the healing process; the mother and child also bathed with water of soaked herbs (such as, *k'boʾx, lɛriyaar, morɛɛt* and *j'maad*); in the case of a stuck placenta, a mother was given a drink made with the *səmluwap sɛgnug* flower.

J'waaŋ

Manaar

When newborn infants experienced *k'laab,* or stomach pain, the *k'laab* plant was sourced to bathe them with and they would also catch the *k'rɛlbool,* or pill millipede, and roll it on the child's body like a marble, so that its smell would help cure the discomfort. Small children who couldn't settle down to sleep were treated with *p'lakoʻoj,* a jungle plant with smooth leaves (similar to *catax*). Its roots, stem and leaves were baked in the fire until burnt and then the ash was made into a paste and smeared onto the child's forehead. In recent times, the *b'ladɛɛr* plant is collected to bath infants with a condition of 'yellowing'.

B'ladɛɛr

K'laab

K'rɛlbool

P'lakoʻoj

Child rashes were treated with the round, shiny *bal* leaf, and *gaas,* or adult skin disorders, could be treated with *b'lɛŋgaŋ.* The sticky sap of the *tampuᵏ* tree was licked in order to cure a mouth ulcer and also the *b'koʻoʻd* fruit (Malay, salak), when still unripe and slightly bitter, was chewed for the same effect. The red fruits of the *laar* leaf, that have edible white pips inside them, were eaten to cure a pustular boil. Another treatment for boils was made with the new leaves of *maŋgoʻoy,* an aubergine variety with small berries (pictured, Vol. 1, p117). The bark of the *t'layax* tree was used to wash skin sores, while *g'lapoh* tree bark and *r'tam* scrapings (of the tall, forest variety, as pictured, Vol. 1, p163, that was used for weaving rice trays) were used to treat acne, and also *campaᵏ,* or chicken pox. Warts were treated with the *kɛlpoʻŋ* fruit, a wild fig (pictured, Vol. 1, p96).

Laar

Bal

B'lɛŋgaŋ

T'layax

Tampuᵏ

Hairy caterpillars, such as *k'maay gííp* or *maməᵏ*, can either give a nasty, painful sting or they can create severe itchiness, with over-heating, nausea and vomiting, and even cause one to pass out. I, myself, have suffered from this, while camping out at the Bərtax River, in 2014, and I didn't even see the caterpillar. My face and tongue swelled up and I became very hot. As it was evening, all they could tell me to do was not to use water, but to stand by the fire and use its heat to bring out the reaction. Normally, to alleviate the irritation, they would rub certain leaves on the body, such as the *g'rōᵏ*, *j'laaᵏ k'maay* or *b'gəəl* leaves. If the sting was very painful, the caterpillar itself would be killed and its insides smeared on the affected area, which would sooth the pain very quickly.

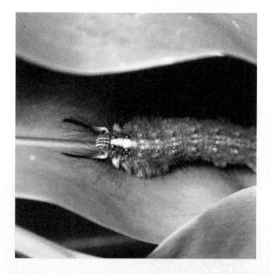

Hairy caterpillars can give a painful sting that causes body heating and swelling.

B'gəəl

J'laaᵏ k'maay

The roots of several plants were known to be effective for pain relief, notably of *p'nag mɔ̃ɔ̃ɲ*, or toothache, including *buŋaaᵏ saguuᵏ*, the canna lily (*Cannaceae canna*), *kɛmbɛl sɛmpoɟy kɛŋkax*, a cloven leaf with 'eyebrows of the horned toad', and *kɛriyax*, a leaf with reddish veins. *Tɛᵏ ʔayaad*, the clay mound often found on the forest floor, made by an emerging cicada, could also be used for curing toothache. *B'raŋsax*, the clay of a wasp nest found in the roof, was made into a paste and smeared on the cheek to reduce inflammation, and even on a woman's breast, to reduce swelling.

The Temiars are also able to source new herbs for treating ailments, which they haven't known before. One such recent find is *ʔagíᵏ*, a grass-like shrub with bright pink flowers, which was brought back from town and planted. Its stems, when cooked and applied to the body, were found to be effective for treating *hɛshiis*, or swelling, such as of the ankles or feet.

Kɛriyax

Kɛmbɛl

Saguuᵏ

Tɛᵏ ʔayaad

B'raŋsax (Credit: ʔAnɛl)

ʔAgíᵏ

Body pain, back pain and muscle pain all had their treatments. The *tɛnruul* root (*Eurycoma longifolia*, known famously by its Malay name, tongkat ali), which lay deep in the ground and could grow as thick as one's leg, was dug up, hacked in pieces and dried, before being boiled to make a herbal tea. It was good for back-ache but also for curing colds. Another one for back ache, as well as fatigue, which they describe as *l'məəs ʔurad*, or weak muscles, was the root and stem of *pɛŋgaar*. Small infants were bathed with it to help them stand and mothers were given it to drink, who felt weak after childbirth. *Tadəəd* (see p1), also, could be drunk to cure back ache. The *cɛŋrɛɛx* leaf was used to rub on sore limbs to ease their pain, after a long walk, for example.

ʔALɨj Sisam, pointing out a tɛnruul tree (tongkat ali) in the forest near Bagan, the root of which is sought after by traders.

Cɛŋrɛɛx

Tɛnruul roots are cut into chips, to be dried and sold to a trader.

Pɛŋgaar

Persons who suffered from breathlessness would cut the buttress of the * haʔoog* tree and make tea from it. Those with chronic breathing problems (including TB) would pull up the fibrous tuber of *k'lawoˈx*, a small yam that grows abundantly in the forest, and make a tea from the dried cuttings. Another usable plant was *sɛdlɔɔd*, that was named after the condition of being breathless. Continual drinking of these herbal teas could help improve their condition.

The Temiars were familiar with a urinary problem which they called *kɛncíŋ manís* (from the Malay term for diabetes, but it was not actually diabetes), which they describe as having difficulty to urinate, and also kidney stones and pain in the kidneys. To cure this condition they chewed the pith of the *catax* plant, and also made a herbal tea with the root of the *k'rudox* bush, which grows rampant in old swiddens.

Ha'oog

K'lawoˈx

Sɛdlɔɔd

Catax

K'lawoˈx root

K'rudox

Another health condition that Temiars suffered from was the inability to do any strenuous work without the eyes blacking out and fainting (in the present day, this is called, *darah tiŋgih*, or high blood pressure). Effective treatments included the bark of *pɛnluᵏ goʹb* (see above), or of *gānyah*, both small trees, and the stems of *misay kucix*, 'cat whiskers', the first of which has been used successfully in recent times, to cure this condition, by two elderly men in Píɲcoʹoŋ village.

Women who desired to cease child-bearing would take certain herbs that were known to pause ovulation, and they would often seek a *halaaᵏ*, or spiritual person, to recite and blow on the herbs so that they would achieve their effect. One well known herb was *manaŋ*, which was so named because it could cause a person to be barren, and others included the *pʉʉt* and *k'ralad* flowers. With the first, the flower bud was eaten or the stem was scraped and made into a drink, but they would need to take much of it in order for it to achieve the intended effect.

The root of the *k'waay b'rayax*, a poisonous yam plant with very irritable sap, was cut thin and inserted into the holes of a woman's ear lobes, to fester them and cause them to widen, so that large decorations could be worn, such as orchids.

Misay kucix

Gānyah

Manaŋ

K'waay b'rayax

Pʉʉd

The montane *pɛnlaay* tree had mystical properties. Its bark was chewed and spat out, and the effect it had was to cause other people, who might be dangerous, to become speechless and run away. *Kasay*, a small plant with fine roots, was pulled up whenever found, and the roots were dried and kept for a later date, to be burned as incense during rituals. For example, they would burn *kasay* root to send off constant rain, when they needed to burn the swidden or go hunting. It would be burned on hot embers during the petitions made at the fruit season or before a dance.

Pɛnlaay tree

The kasay plant; its root was dried and burned as incense during petitions and at ritual dances.

K'míɲam, a sweet incense, was obtained from a tree of the same name, by scraping its resin. It was burned at burials.

Certain animal bones were also used in medications, sometimes for treating illnesses caused by *sabat* animals (mentioned in Vol. 1, p82), but also for other situations. *J'ʔɛŋ ʔamɔɔ^k* or the bones of serow (mountain goat) were burned and made into a paste and applied to an expectant mother's womb, or mixed in water and drunk by her, to enable her to give birth easily. It is told in the Temiar folk tales that the mountain goat was the *tulag*, or midwife, who helped the first woman give birth, and it told them that whenever they ate its meat they should keep its bones, to be used to help women give birth.

Sɛgnug kɛŋkax, the horned toad, was eaten in the old days as a cure for a cold, as its eggs were bitter and had a good effect. Today, *dɛmdup*, or river newts, are eaten when one suffers a cold, and they also taste quite bitter.

The eggs of the kɛŋkax toad were a cure for a cold.

The white resin of the gooc tree was used for treating mouth ulcers.

Condition	Description	Herbal Remedies
pijɛd ʔɛij, hɛbhaab, r'waac	stomach aches and diarrhea	*g'lapoh, k'bəəᵏ kolím, paɲííl, tadəəd, taŋhoʼy, tɛɛx g'woʼm, tɛɛx kadɔɔᵏ-daax, tɛɛx pasùg*
bʉd ʔulah	high temperature and fever	*ʔapoʼʂ ləwɛɛy, ʔancōōʼᵏ/ k'lupaᵏ, baay, buŋaaᵏ carax, cɛdroʼʼd pantɛy, cɛlcoʼʼl, galox, hənaroox, jaram, jɛrnaŋ, k'boʼx, lɛmpoʼʼj, lɛmpux, lɛriyaar, morɛɛt, pɛnyaaw (laŋɛɛd), riyɛɛs lalaŋ, r'tam, tɛɛx c'moʼg, taliᵏ manoʼw, ti²ux (bamboo water), toʼʼx (bamboo chalk)*
sùᵏwad	colds	*ʔapoʼʂ bahoʼʼᵏ, bayuur, boʼʼd bɛmhup, cihuŋ, s'dùx, tɛnruul, sɛgnug kɛŋkax (horned toad), dɛmdup (newts)*
jɛᵏjiiᵏ	general illness	*bɛrdaax, cadag, cɛgloʼg, cihuŋ, galox, j'maad, moŋlɛɛy, moʼʼŋ*
tɛŋoʼʼr kuuy	migraines	*ʔapoʼʂ kɛŋwoʼʼx, s'laaᵏ bɛjsíj, tabaar*
loyɛc	dizziness	*kayaaᵏ, p'lakoʼʼj, ʔuloʼx*
sabat	illness caused by taboo animals	*jaram, soʼʼg boʼt, taroʼg*
na-gəd, maŋkɛy	cuts and wounds	*ʔakoʼw, balùd, bərcaap, cɛdroʼʼd, cɛgloʼg, jaay mamoʼᵏ, sɛŋkoʼᵏ ʔawɛn ʔaloʼʼy, taŋhoʼy*
nɛscuus	burns	*cadít*
raŋyɛ̄ᵏ	post-natal care	*bal, bəər k'laab, j'waaŋ, kacíp, mamoʼᵏ, pɛnluᵏ goʼb, səmluwap sɛgnug*
saŋɛ̄ɛ̄d b'ladɛɛr	yellow babies	*b'ladɛɛr*
k'laab	infants with gall pain	*k'laab, k'rɛlbool*
bataᵏ	child rashes	*s'laaᵏ bal, sɛŋkoʼᵏ laŋsad (langsat tree bark)*
gaas	scabies	*b'lɛŋgaŋ*
bɛjsíj k'maay	poisonous caterpillar stings	*b'gəəl, s'laaᵏ g'rō̄ᵏ, s'laaᵏ jalaaᵏ k'maay*
k'mɔɔn, campaᵏ	acne, chicken pox	*g'lapoh, r'tam bɛɛx*

Condition	Description	Herbal Remedies
k'sɛɛd	warts	*k'bəə^k kɛlpo̓ŋ*
sɛl	boils	*k'bəə^k laar, s'laa^k maŋgo̓o̓y*
na-hoor gɛntóx	ear infection	*bɔɔ^k ʔasaad* (the stem of squash plant)
p'nag mõ̃õ̃ɲ	toothache	*buŋaa^k saguu^k, kɛmbɛl sɛmpóy kɛŋkax, kɛriyax*
pijɛd ʔurad	muscle pain	*cɛŋrɛɛx*
pijɛd k'rə^k	backache	*pɛŋgaar, p'nugas/tɛnruul* (tongkat ali), *tadəəd*
nɛshīīs	inflammation	*b'raŋsax* (hornet nest), *buŋaa^k ʔagí^k, cɛdro̓o̓d, tɛ^k ʔayaad* (cicada mound)
pijɛd kɛlkɛɛl	joint pain	*cɛdro̓o̓d*
silo̓ic	sprains	*balùd, b'rɛlnyo̓o̓l*
darah tíŋgih	high blood pressure	*gānyah, misay kucix, pɛnlu^k go̓b*
sɛdlɔɔd	breathlessness	*cantɛŋ haʔoog, pɛnlu^k go̓b, sɛdlɔɔd, t'layax*
TB	tuberculosis	*k'lawo̓x*
kɛncíŋ manís	urinary problems	*catax, k'ludox*
bɛhbəəh	male stimulant	*carɛŋ, tɛnruul*
lɛsməəs ʔurad	weakness	*pɛŋgaar, taŋsiih*
jɛ^k kɛswēēs	to end child-bearing	*buŋaa^k k'ralad, buŋaa^k pʉʉt, manaŋ*
cɛ^k	head lice	*buŋaa^k b'laŋaa^k*
cacíŋ	intestinal worms	*kolím*
lɛblaab mad	to wash the face	*jarííj*

Table 7. Summary of herbal medicines used by the Temiars.

Betel nut was a fruit that the Temiars could hardly go without, probably due to it being so addictive, and was chewed by young and old alike, as a relaxant or energiser. But *pinaŋ*, or areca nut (*Areca catechu*), a round-shaped and rock-hard palm seed, which is popular throughout South and Southeast Asia, was only planted by the Temiars in the last hundred years. Originally, they would collect *k'bəaᵏ j'roˊx*, or *k'bəaᵏ l'goˊog*, the fruits of small palms that could be found in the higher, cooler forest. These small, oval fruits had much the same effect as the common areca (Malay, pinang), in that they made one's head light, but the chewing was also said to strengthen one's teeth and they will point to old people who chewed it all their lives and still have their teeth intact.

As with the Malays, betel was rarely chewed alone (except when walking in the mountains and finding fruit-laden *j'roˊx* palms to be picked) and they would prepare pieces of *kalox*, a vine, or the *bəyaad* or *kacuuᵏ* leaves (Malay, sirih and gambeh), to chew with the nut and add flavour. If they had lime paste then this would be smeared on the leaves before the betel was wrapped up in them and this would add density and also turn their mouths red. When a mouthful was fully chewed and had lost its spice, then the mix was spat out, through the gaps in the floor if they sat in the house, to spatter the ground underneath with many patches of red. To obtain the lime they collected *k'bəaᵏ kapur*, or 'chalk fruit' (a taboo avoidance term for *katoŋ*, or black river snails), from certain small streams and, after extracting the meat for consumption, the calcareous shells were pounded. The Píŋcoˊoŋ River actually obtained its name from the snail shell pounding (expressed as '*coˊoŋ-coˊoŋ*') that once took place there, at the Kapur River, near Taaᵏ Kabɛl's cave.

J'roˊx

L'goˊog

The late Pəŋhuluᵏ P'diᵏ and ²Alʉj Soïd collect betel nut fruits from the old orchard at Sapɛd.

6 | *SAKAA^k*: TEMIAR CUSTOMARY LAND

6.1   A DEFINITION OF *SAKAA^k*

The principle of Temiar *sakaa^k* is perhaps similar to the traditional Malay principle of saka, from where the name in Temiar originates. The word can be used to describe anything that is owned due to historical rights to it, whether it be a coconut tree planted by one's grandfather, or the land where one's ancestors dwelt and were buried. It can also describe something that was owned and has since gone, such as a necklace someone bought when making a memorable journey years ago. In terms of land, we can further define what the word fully encompasses in the Temiar mind:

One's sakaa^k is the land passed down from the tɛ^ktaa^k manah (forefathers) of one's k'mo͝om (kin group), which extends from the main-river of their domain until the farthest reaches of that river's watershed (the ridge-line surrounding the river valley), of which those ancestors were spiritual guardians, and from which they sustained their lives, and which they entrusted to the guardianship of their descendants after them.

The oldest known tataa^k manah or forefather of the Temiars of the Bərtax River region (who now live at Tɛmagaa^k village, at Pos Gɔɔb) was Taa^k Galoŋ.[1] He settled at Tajaar, in the land of the Bərtax River (see Fig. 4, p36), in the late 19th Century, and cut swiddens along the south side of the river. He dwelt together with compatriots such as Taa^k K'rundoŋ, Taa^k J'rɛŋkaŋ and Taa^k Tawix, three other forefathers of the Puyan Temiar.

The whole land of the Upper Puyan and Bərtax Rivers was their domain, even as far down as the Puyan river-mouth, on the Jɛnro͝l River. They made swiddens in any suitable location and hunted and fished, and gathered fruits, wild ferns and herbal medicines to sustain the lives of their families in any part of the land that they considered theirs to roam. That is, they did not make hunting trips into the neighbouring valleys, such as at the R'ko͝ob River (westward) or the Bayuur River (eastward), even though they did walk over to the long-houses in those valleys for social visits. Sometimes they rafted down the Puyan to enjoy the good fishing at the Jɛnro͝l River, but that's because the river was large, fish were plentiful, and to tɛsgo͝os, or sustain life, from the main river was not considered encroaching on another Temiar's domain.

6.1 Taa^k Galoŋ came from the Bəər region (at the B'ro͝ox River source), which is said to be where the Temiar people originated from, and is called, ʔAsal Gɛrlo͝ox.

The sons of these early forefathers, especially Taa^k ʔAmpís, son of Taa^k Galoŋ, continued their fathers' control of their domain by planting swiddens, hunting, fishing, gathering, and walking far and wide on the mountains in search of herbs and materials, while also encountering the souls of nature inhabiting the land in their dreams. They in turn entrusted their domains to their own children, to roam and to cultivate. They warned their children and grand-children not to forsake their land or surrender it to outsiders. It was sacred to them; they had met the souls of the land in their dreams, from whom the rights to live there had been bestowed, together with all its life-giving resources.

The late Pəŋhulu^k P'di^k, at his home, in 2014.

²Ɛlan P'di^k, son of the late Pəŋhulu^k P'di^k, who lives today at Tɛmagaa^k.

Today, the great-grand-children of Pəŋhulu^k P'di^k K'lusar, of Tɛmagaa^k village, are eight generations from Taa^k Galoŋ. They are the children of ²Amri, son of ²Ɛlan, son of P'di^k, son of K'lusar, son of P'naŋơw, son of ²Ampís, son of Galoŋ.

The Temiars of Tɛmagaa^k say that, true to the above definition, Taa^k K'lusar, entrusted the land of the Bərtax to his children and grand-children before he died. They call this land their *sakaa^k j'nơm*, which means the land, with its resources, fruit trees and swiddens, of their birth. They also call members of the same *k'mơơm*, or kin group, their *sakɛy*, persons who share rights to the same *sakaa^k* (which is in contrast to the derogatory term 'sakai', meaning slave, used in times past to describe the Temiars).

Soïd mountain, which rising high over the land of the Bərtax River.

(Credit: ꞌArí Kɛnto̓n)

From the highest reaches of the Bərtax River, a view from Síríŋ mountain toward So̓id.

The forested land of the Upper Puyan River.

The view of Bərlɛy mountain, from So̓id, which stands behind today's Tɛmagaaᵏ and most of the old settlements.

It has been stated by others that the word *sakaaᵏ* stands only for the 'possessions' of the forefathers in their customary land, mainly the swiddens and fruit trees that they planted, or the trees from which they harvested fruits or tapped latex. These swiddens and trees, that bear the names of the original planters and finders until today, were passed down to successive generations as possessions or *sakaaᵏ*.

This however is only a partial picture of what the word implies in the custom of the Temiars. As stated above, *sakaaᵏ* also stands for the land in which the forefathers of a particular kin group settled, roamed and found their spiritual home. The trees that they planted, whether durian, jias, pinang or even blow-pipe bamboo, and the trees that they frequented, such as *sɛmpaaᵏ* (jungle durian), *do̓og* (the blow-dart poison tree), *Bado̓ox* (native rubber), *gꞌtah cɛp* (bird-gum tree) and many more, were indeed inheritable 'possessions' that each kin group laid claim to. Though it is not only these, for the graves of the forefathers and places of significance, such as the caves where people fled for refuge during times of danger, are also considered *sakaaᵏ*.

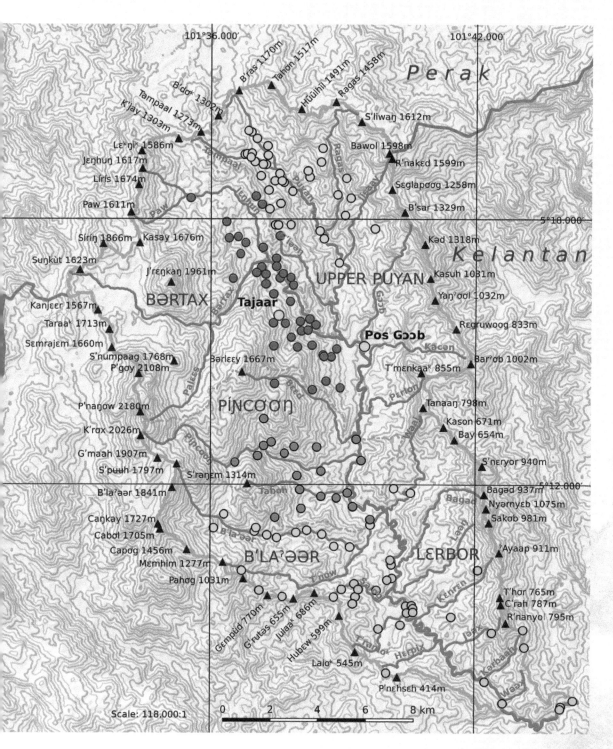

Fig. 4. Map showing the dispersal of the pre-1950 swiddens, on the Upper Puyan, Bərtax, Píŋcʊ́oŋ, B'la²əər and Lower Puyan Rivers, with the surrounding ring of mountains which make the boundary of today's Pos Gɔɔb territory. The dashed green lines demarcate the boundaries between the river zones or ancestral land (sakaaᵏ) of the different Temiar kin groups.

Their ancestors did not arrive looking for a good place to plant crops, as if they were in a trading business! They came looking for land to roam, with game to hunt, and they claimed the land with its river, which to them was the heart and life of the land. They dwelt wherever they desired along their river, having complete freedom, as the river was their limit. It would be quite illogical to say that they only claimed the land that they cultivated, as, obviously, they could only cut one or two swiddens at a time. While a swidden was providing crops, the rest of the valley lay available, for any suitable site to be cultivated at a future date. The cutting of swiddens, therefore, was evidence that they claimed the river valley, and thus a kin group's *sakaa^k* today cannot be reduced to the old swiddens and planted trees alone, it must find the same limits that their ancestors had, which are those of the river. The river valley, with its swiddens and resources, is considered their *sakaa^k* (this concept was originally put forward by H. D. Noone, 1936, but was later rebutted by Benjamin, 1968[2]). When the different *sakaa^k* (in practical terms, neighbouring river valleys) are considered as a whole, they are then described as *tε^k sεŋro'x*, or land of the Temiars.

The main river would normally be a large tributary of the 'mother river', such as the Bərtax, Pȋŋco'oŋ or B'la²əər Rivers, or else it could be the river source area of the 'mother river' such as with the Upper Puyan. The land on the lower river may be another kin group's *sakaa^k*, as with the Lower Puyan and its tributaries. The *sakaa^k* of the Bərtax River's kin group does not cross the geographical boundary into the Puyan valley eastward, as this is the *sakaa^k* of the Puyan River's kin group, whose forefather was Taa^k Panda^k, a Temiar from Perak, who married into the family of Taa^k ²Ampís. With him were contemporaries Taa^k Ranah and Taa^k Ramo'y, who roamed in the land of the Upper Puyan River. Today, their descendants live at Gɔɔb, Kacəŋ, B'ro'g and Bərcaap villages (see Fig. 5, p54).

6.2 Headmanship And Leadership In Temiar Society (1968), p2.

Brahím P'di^k stands at the confluence of the Bərtax with the Puyan, the lowland boundary between the two kin groups of these rivers.

Samsudín B'kəd stands at the mouth of the Bɛɛd River, the boundary of the Píncơo̊ŋ and Bərtax River regions.

The Puyan River at Lamớg, the boundary between the Píncơo̊ŋ and B'la²əər regions.

Standing on Capaaᵏ mountain, at the Píncơo̊ŋ-Bərtax boundary.

Standing at Soh hill, on the boundary between the Bərtax with the Puyan.

ˀAríf Pandaᵏ, standing on the ridge near Pɛrsuud mountain, points down toward the source of the Palɛɛs River.

Standing at Batuᵏ Jaŋkar, at the Píɲcơoŋ-B'laˀəər boundary.

Normally, Temiars from the Bərtax River kin group would not hunt or gather in the *sakaaᵏ* of the Puyan River kin group, and vice-versa. They definitely would not venture to plant swiddens or collect forest trade products, such as rattan, inside another kin group's *sakaaᵏ*. But as resources are now more scarce, it is possible that Bərtax Temiars will venture high up the Puyan for a day or two, and it is typical that Temiars from both these groups use the lower stretches of the Puyan River for fishing.

The forefathers of the Píɲcơoŋ River kin group, Taaᵏ Kabɛl, Taaᵏ B'jun and Taaᵏ K'naɲlow, likewise entrusted the land to their descendants, and the Temiars living today at Pinaŋ village (known as Píɲcơoŋ), remain the rightful owners of that *sakaaᵏ* according to their custom. Outsiders can only occupy parts of this land by marriage into the Píɲcơoŋ clan, as some Temiars from the Bərtax, the Jɛnrơl and Lɛmpar Rivers have done. The same can be said of Temiars further down the Puyan River, living at Tanjuŋ, Gawíín, Calɛɛr and Guwaaɲ villages, who are descended from the forefathers who dwelt at the B'laˀəər and Lɛrbor Rivers, and in the land toward the Puyan river-mouth. They are the rightful owners of the Lower Puyan *sakaaᵏ*.

When a Temiar from either one of these groups living in today's villages is asked, "What is your *sakaaᵏ*?", without hesitation they will tell you it is their river, and the land that contains it, including the swiddens which their ancestors cut, the trees that they planted, the mountains and rivers that they saw in their dreams and gave names to, the whole domain where they roamed and gathered, and over which they were made guardians.

Kudín ʔAŋah points to a clump of sᵊwo̓o̓r blowpipe bamboo growing on Sᵊwo̓o̓r peak, on the path up to So̓id.

Manau rattan is prepared for collection by Temiars of the Upper Puyan kin group, in 2014..

Temiars of the Bərtax kin group prepare to catch fish in their river.

Fruit trees at Tagoŋ, which have survived around 50 years, are part of the Pĩ́ncoʼoŋ kin group's sakaaᵏ.

A jiyɛɛs tree that was planted by Kɛntoʼn ʔAloŋ, of the Puyan kin group, many years ago.

An old durian tree at Pĩ́ncoʼoŋ stands as testimony to the ancestors who planted it.

A rambɛy tree (rambai), at Rɛnloŋ, as thick as hardwood after so many years. (Credit: Rapi)

6.2 THE ORIGINS OF PLACE NAMES IN THE PUYAN VALLEY

6.2.1 Our Investigation Of Primary Names

The origin of place names in the Temiar territories can be traced back a few hundred years to the venerable ancestors of today's inhabitants, the Tataaᵏ Bɛlyans, who held an ancient knowledge of the spirit world. These early dwellers walked the length and breadth of the land and also saw it in their dreams, and they ascribed names to every mountain, hill, valley and river as they deemed fit. These names have been passed down from one generation to another, and are still used by today's Temiars, so that whenever they need to describe where they saw langurs in the forest or where they will go to cut rattan, they recall the ancient stories. Only a few places have been named more recently, since the return from the gathering and relocation downriver, over 50 years ago, but most originate from the Tataaᵏ Bɛlyans.

From some 1650 places that were mapped by the community of Pos Gɔɔb in their territory, I was able to list over a thousand Temiar names with their meanings (refer to the full list of names in Appendix 2). The list is not an exhaustive one however, as there are undoubtedly many hills that were not climbed, and gullies and rivers that were not marked by the mappers, as time and energy did not permit. But I have collected enough names to discover some very interesting trends of Temiar customary naming, which are not only of special linguistic interest, but they reveal how greatly the Temiars are bonded with their land and how they cared to link every place with species, events and customs that were important to them. Today's inhabitants keep a mental map of where all these places are, and hold them as a sacred part of their heritage, showing that they are indeed heirs of the land to which their ancestors first ascribed all those names.

Digging up the meanings of these names was no easy task either. It took much perseverance, with hours and hours of investigation, until we were frequently worn out, as they detailed what they knew and tried to recall what they had forgotten. We returned again and again to the list, in order to fill in the gaps and to discover a clearer picture of others. Many times, the stories they told didn't seem to make any sense, and especially because they expected me to know half of the story beforehand, including Temiar words that I hadn't heard before, or the names of trees, fruits, birds, plants, or the customs that they knew by heart. It took persistence to extract the true story, as it was so easy for them to say, it's called X because X happened there, while by-passing the actual meaning of 'X'. When I thought I had conquered the task pretty well, someone took my list of names and started marking my errors, which had accumulated due to plentiful misunderstandings. Following that, in 2019, I checked another 150 Temiar words in the list with the Temiars of Píɲcơơŋ and we were able to clear up an equal number of errors.

The list contains all the places I consider to have primary names, which are those places named from certain circumstances. Thus, there are another 600 or more places that acquired their name from these places with primary names, due to their geographic relationship. Sometimes a swidden was named after the nearby river or hill (e.g. Bagan, Gɛrhaar), or a river or hill was named after the swidden (e.g. Soh hill, from Soh, a favourite hunters' camp). In the case of the name coming from a particular human activity, then the origin of the name would certainly come from the swidden. But in the case of the name originating from a tree, flower, plant or ant species, for example, then either river, hill or swidden might have been named first.

The inter-connectivity between place names becomes apparent once we have collected the geographic points of a whole area of Temiar land. Hills and mountains are often named after the river that has its source in them (Tampaal, Waaj, B′la²əər), but also rivers can be named after the hill from which they flow (Soɨd, Paw, K′jaay, Ragas, Pɛnrɛɛw, K′lɛɛr). It depends on which was named first or which was prominent in the stories or dreams. But there are rivers that have no hill or mountain named after them, for example, Kacəŋ, Puyan, Píɲcɔ́ɔ́ŋ and many others. A large waterfall on a small river will likely carry the name of the river, such as Kacəŋ or Camɛɛŋ, but due to there being numerous waterfalls on some rivers, many of them have names characteristic of themselves, such as the cascading of water on rocks, or of trees and fauna found nearby.

Luwag gɛrgug, named after the hill, which was named because of frogs making a "gug-gug" sound.

Risut ²Adiᵏ stands at a luwag, or mountain pass, at the border with Perak.

A *jɛlmoˊl* is typically described as a high point on a mountain or mountain chain, of which, in the latter case, there can be multiple *jɛlmoˊl* joined together, but the highest peak of a mountain is called a *t'pas*. Where there is a more visually free-standing mountain, the mountain as a whole will take on the name of the predominant peak. For example, Jɛlmoˊl Soˊid speaks of the entire mountain which has four main peaks, with Soˊid being one of them (but not technically the highest). Jɛlmoˊl Bərlɛɛy also contains multiple peaks, but the highest and the one with greatest significance, from where they collect the shiny blowpipe bamboo, is Bərlɛɛy peak.

A *taŋkoˊl* is described as a high point in any place, either of a hill, a rise along a ridge, or a rise in low-land areas. For lack of an English word I use 'gully' to describe *luwag*, which is not a gully in the sense of a recessed river bed. It is either a cutting through a ridge, sometimes as a narrow pathway through the rock from one side to the other, or sometimes as a 30-80 foot deep dip all the way through. In lower areas, the *luwag* is often a much wider dip in the land. *Luwag* are found at river sources, but perpendicular to the river and without flowing water. They are important landmarks, as well as passes through areas of raised land. Gullies are named after the mountain peak nearest them, or the hill or river if in the lower valleys. Caves have usually been named after the swiftlets and bats which nest in them, but sometimes after the river, a plant or even a person who died there.

Tɛŋkoˊh Ləruw, the largest waterfall in the region, was named after the soul of the waterfall., who was seen in a dream.

Two Temiars from Píɲcoˊoŋ take a rest on the peak of Kamar mountain, while walking along the boundary of their land.

Guwɔɔᵏ Taaᵏ Kabɛl, a cave at the Píɲcoˊoŋ River that was named after an ancestor who died there. (Credit: Rapi)

6.2.2　Categorisation Of Name Origins

From the thousand primary toponyms and their meanings (including some 80 or so duplicate names derived from popular species), I was able to create some 25 categories of name origin. Eight of these categories are grouped under plant species, four under animal species, two under environmental conditions, seven under human factors and events, and the last four under non-human factors.

Over half of the names (55%), come under the first group, those derived from natural species of trees and plants, while almost a quarter were from the second and third groups (13% and 12% respectively), of animals and birds, and from environmental conditions such as the shape of the land and the weather. Thus over three quarters (78%) of all place names originate from sources of nature—which is perhaps a good indication of the Temiars' attachment to the natural environment.

The largest category, comprising almost 190 names, was of forest trees, and mostly of hardwood species. Adding to this 110 names derived from wild fruit trees used by hunters, and another 52 names from edible fruit trees, the total number of names derived from trees comes to 350, or a third (35%) of all the names recorded. Thus it is clear that trees played a significant role in Temiar place naming, which was likely due to their physical prominence in the forest and the fact that the majority of trees are so well identified by the Temiars. Interestingly, names derived from trees make up a third or more of most place type names: of swiddens, 37%, of mountains, 20%, of hills, 49%, of gullies, 32%, of rivers, 30%, of waterfalls, 27% and of river pools, 54%. The percentage of mountain names derived from trees is lower due to a higher share of names being derived from flower species, the environment and dreams.

Names derived from human factors, from encounters with souls, catastrophes and events in dreams—or from sources other than nature—gave rise to a fifth of all names (20%). Dreams however should not be passed over as a small factor in naming of places, as certain other factors, such as environment, animal, or custom, that names were derived from, were seen in dreams, not in waking life.

GROUP 1: CATEGORIES OF NATURAL SPECIES

Tree and Plant Species (8 categories)

The presence of certain species in the area, of tree, plant, vine, bamboo, fruit, flower, or herb, either significant in size, prominence, abundance, or of traditional value such as medicinal plants or fragrant leaves collected for the dances.

- Taŋko̍l Kolím (Kolím Hill), named after the *kolím* tree.
- ʔO̍o̍x Pɨɨn (Pɨɨn River), named after the *pɨɨt* flower.

Animals and Birds (4 categories)

Notably, the presence (and nuisance) of the tiger, other animals heard or encountered, such as the civet, the pangolin, a rhinoceros, a bear or the call of an owl or other bird. Encounters with biting ants, wasps or centipedes. Fish or frogs that were caught at the river.

- Taŋkoɩ Balíŋ (Balíŋ Hill), a tiger was met here, and *balíŋ* is a name for the tiger.
- Tɛŋkoh Tayaas (Tayaas Waterfall), named after an otter that bit through a fish trap and took the fish.

GROUP 2: CATEGORIES OF THE ENVIRONMENT

Natural Environment

The area may have certain physical features, such as being steep, or rocky, or narrow or wide of space, or being curved, straight or truncated. Even the rubbing together of two trees, the hitting together of blow-pipe bamboo on the mountain, the spatter of water from a waterfall on the rocks or its tumbling into a pool, or a rainbow could give name to a place. Perhaps something profound or unusual happened when a group of hunters reached a certain river, such as the sky turned red at evening.

- Jɛlmoɩ Lɛntííŋ (Lɛntííŋ Mountain), from *p'rɛndííŋ*, which means straight.
- ʔOox Cɛghaag (Cɛghaag River), the waterfall at this river makes a *c'rɛghaag* pounding sound.

Weather

The sky turned black with rain clouds, it blew there with a gusty wind or the hill was shrouded with mist.

- Taŋkoɩ S'rikɔɔb (S'rikɔɔb Hill), the sky was dark with rain clouds; from *s'rikɔɔb*, darkening.
- ʔOox Pataag (Pataag River), the rain dripped from the trees; *sɛgpataag*, dripping.

GROUP 3: CATEGORIES OF HUMAN FACTORS

Events that took place

An old man's loin cloth caught fire, they gathered together for fear of a tiger, they went bat-hunting or they were stuffing yam into bamboo tubes. An old woman and her house were transported onto a mountain-top.

- Jɛlmoɩ Rɛnupoɩw (Rɛnupoɩw Mountain), from *rɛmupoɩw*, popping of bamboo in the fire.
- ʔOox Jɛŋhuŋ (Jɛŋhuŋ River), a bamboo tube fell onto a rock making a gong sound, *g'rahooŋ*.

Feeling

During a long walk they felt tired, hungry, cold, or they felt wonder when reaching a mountain-top, as if the earth had moved.

- Gɛrbɔɔ^k B'goɩŋ (B'goɩŋ Ridge), there was no water and they were thirsty; *pɛŋp'goɩŋ*, thirsty.

Person

A Temiar was born there, died there, frequented the pool for fishing or fell in into a whirlpool and couldn't get out! The place then took the name of that person.

- Síntam (swidden), Sintam ʔAnjaŋ, was born at the swidden.
- Luwag Lagol (Lagol Gully), a bald man ran from a bear; *lagol*, bald.

Man-made items

A betel nut bowl was dropped at a waterfall, a knife sheath was dropped and lost, a spear was dropped and it transmogrified into a rock. A bronze bracelet was found, or a nose flute was made there.

- Taŋkɔ́l Tarɔ́g (Tarɔ́g Hill), there is wood here to make spear shafts; *tarɔ́g*, spear.
- Gool B'laŋaaᵏ (B'laŋaaᵏ Pool), they dropped a *b'laŋaaᵏ*, or wok, from the raft in this pool.

Crops and food (2 categories)

They had a good millet harvest which brought them great happiness, or they had a bumper crop of gourds. Sometimes they had food with them on a journey that went bad, or was bitter.

- Jawaᵏ (swidden), they planted millet; *jawaᵏ*, millet.
- Lacaaŋ (swidden), they boiled manioc and it went soft and sticky; *b'lacaaŋ*, translucent.

Customs

A petition was made to plead for the storm to cease, they were talking about rat-trapping, or women were collecting flowers to stuff in the hair.

- C'nɔɔs (swidden), they burned *kasay* root, in order to hold off the rain; *c'nɔɔs*, ritual prayer.
- ʔỚox Bajaax (Bajaax River), they built rat-trapping hut, called a *bajaax*.

GROUP 4: CATEGORIES OF NON-CONTROLLABLE FACTORS

Spiritual

A bərbơw tree demanded them to make an offering, in order for it to cool its anger, or a man slept and a mountain soul caught his soul away, a woman was held captive by a Jaaᵏ ʔAwooy, or a medium received a token of power from a soul in a dream.

- Layan (swidden), they offered blood to the *bɛrbơw* tree; *layan*, to offer.
- Badớox Taaᵏ Gɛndow (Jelutong tree of Taaᵏ Gɛndow), Taaᵏ ʔAmpís sent the soul of a malevolent tiger into this *badớox* tree.

Catastrophe

A storm arose and rocks came down and buried a group of travelers, or the earth turned over and consumed a party of children who had teased a monkey.

- Lɛŋraaŋ (swidden), the earth turned over and consumed a group of Menriqs; *lɛŋlaaŋ*, earthquake.
- Taŋkɔ́l Lɛgliig (Lɛgliig Hill), a storm blew up at midday; *lɛgliig*, consuming.

Deaths

A man was killed by a tiger and his blood congealed on the rocks, and another man died of hunger and was found crawling on all-fours.

- Gɛrbɔɔᵏ C'rɛŋkap (C'rɛŋkap Ridge), Gɛslas Mɛndol died on Soid mountain; *c'rɛŋkap*, a crawl.
- J'rəp L'bíír (L'bíír Gorge) Taaᵏ Solah, a Jehai, was attacked by a tiger; *k'baar*, to clot, changed to L'bíír.

Dreams

The Tataaᵏ Bɛlyans followed their dream-guide to different parts of the land, and they named places according to what they had seen there.

- Jɛlmoʼl S'numpaag (S'numpaag Mountain), the tiger guníg of Taaᵏ ²Ampís swore an oath; *s'numpaag*, an oath.
- Gool Jəəx (Jəəx Pool), a man dreamed of a crocodile and its name was Jəəx.

The last category, names derived from dreams, is perhaps the most interesting as there are not many peoples in the world who have the custom of naming places from encounters in dreams. The dream-guide guníg led its master all over the land and thus the Tataaᵏ Bɛlyan saw many of its features and knew of places even before he had ventured there on foot. He would also see the guníg acting in certain ways, like singing a Temiar song, or meet with a pət'rii soul, the dominant soul of the mountain, and discover their names from his guníg. When he awoke he would tell of these dreams in the long-house and ascribe names to those places where he had been.

The view from Soʼid, down over the Bərtax River.

7 | ORIGINS AND ANCESTRY OF THE PUYAN TEMIARS

The territory of Pos Gɔɔb today comprises some twelve villages dotted along the Puyan River, with five around Gɔɔb itself, two more further down, at the Píɲcơơŋ River, two more at the B′la²əər River and the last three being situated near the Kɛnrɛn River. The land itself is divided into four large regions, each being home to a different *k'moơm*, or kin group, of Temiars, descended from the forefathers who first settled those valleys (see Fig. 5, p54). The Temiars of today's villages still maintain life through the resources of their own *sakaaᵏ*, or hereditary land, and do not encourage anyone foraging in river valleys other than their own. The Temiars of Tɛmagaaᵏ village, on the hill facing across the river from Pos Gɔɔb, have their roots in the Bərtax River region, to the north-west. The Temiars living at Gɔɔb, with three other villages nearby, have their roots in the Upper Puyan region, to the north. Those living at Pinaŋ have their roots in the Píɲcơơŋ river region, in the mid-west of the land, and those at Gawíín with its villages both in the B′la²əər River and Lower Puyan region, to the south of the land.

Therefore, in the following summary of ancestry, I now look at the origins of these present-day Temiars of the Puyan valley, going back to their pre-war history (pre-1954), to discover where their ancestors dwelt in the land. In the following two chapters, I look at what happened to them as individual kin groups during the war years (the Emergency of the 1950s-60s and their relocation downriver) and the period immediately afterwards, when moderate stability was restored (up to the 1970s) and they began to resettle their homeland, moving around in their own valleys once more.

7.1   KAMPUɄ TƐMAGAAᵏ

The majority of families living at Tɛmagaaᵏ village are descended from an ancestor named **Taaᵏ Galoŋ**, and those Temiars who were contemporary with him.

These ancestors first shifted to the tributary rivers of the Bərtax close to 160 years ago. Their sons with their families explored and inhabited more land, finding suitable dwelling places in the deep undisturbed forest on the upper reaches of the Puyan River, and also over the mountain border from there at the S′ŋaaᵏ River, in Perak. Some of them also moved down-river to the Lɛrbor on the Lower Puyan (see Fig. 6, pre-1950s swiddens of the Bərtax River, p61).

7.1.1   Tɛmagaaᵏ: Taaᵏ Galoŋ

Taaᵏ Galoŋ is the furthest ancestor of the late Pəŋhuluᵏ P′diᵏ who can be remembered (see the ancestry of Tɛmagaaᵏ, Fig. 7). He must have been born in the 19th Century, as he is four generations before Pəŋhuluᵏ P′diᵏ. His only son was **²Ampís**. His daughter, **²Aŋah**, died while young.

He resided in the area of the **Kɛmbʉ**ᵏ and **Sirah** Rivers, and made dwellings at **Tajaar**, **T'lor,** **S'rijøʻh**, **Kaləŋ**, **Sigaŋ**, **S'poʻy**, **Siyaduh**, **Calyɛx**, and **Papan**. These places are the oldest swiddens in the history of the Puyan River Temiars.

Taaᵏ Galoŋ came to the Bərtax River looking for fish, which were plentiful in those days. Jehais inhabited the land of the Puyan valley at the time. Later on, it is said, the Jehais handed over care of the land to Taaᵏ Galoŋ and they moved back to Perak.

He is known to have roamed about the entire land of the Bərtax and Puyan, hunting and fishing. He was a Tataaᵏ Bɛlyan and met with soul-guides in his dreams. He could also invoke souls of nature in the Temiar *nɛhpɔɔh*, ritual dances. He understood much of the land through his dreams and also named several places, although not as many as his son named from his dreams.

*Bawə ꞌAdi*ᵏ *picks ferns at the Kɛmbʉ*ᵏ *River, near Tajaar.*

View from the Bərtax River down toward Sakoʻb Mountain, midway down the Puyan valley.

His grave site is located at **Taŋkoˀl Tajaar** (Tajaar Hill), near **S'rijoˀh**. It must be noted that with many 'burials' in the old days, the body was placed above ground in a burial hut, called a *paax*, so there is no visible dip in the ground, unlike with many recent burials which show a notable dip in the ground, made from the collapsed bamboo coffin. The ancestors were afraid to dig the ground or afraid that the soul would return to the place to haunt it if the body was in the ground.

The grave site of Taaᵏ Galoŋ, a distant ancestor of the Temiars.

An old tree stump at Sigaŋ and a logging road going through Papan. (Credit: ˀIdrís ˀAsod)

Calyɛx

7.1.2 Tɛmagaaᵏ: Taaᵏ K'rundơŋ

Taaᵏ K'rundơŋ was a contemporary of Taaᵏ Galoŋ, and another great ancestor of the Bərtax Temiars. His sons were **Tukaŋ**, and one other who died at **Cɔɔs cave** (the Malay name is Gua Cha), during the gathering by the British Army. He lived at **Tagat**, **Calyɛx**, **P'rawas** and **S'tool**. His grave can be found at the **Tagat** River where he had lived.

Two other Temiar contemporaries of Taaᵏ Galoŋ were **Taaᵏ K'caaw** (his real name ?Adiᵏ ?Alaŋ) who lived at **K'caaw, K'mơơᵏ, Pakuᵏ, Cakob, Tayug,** and **T'ramơᵏ**, and **Taaᵏ Rɛwrơơw** (who's real name is unknown) who lived at **Rɛwrơơw, ?Entɛɛb**, and **Jɛrhooh**.

Tukaŋ K'rundơŋ knew how to shape scrap iron and make tools such as the hooked knife, called the *?awaaj wɛɛɲ*, and thus he was called Tukaŋ, or smith. He had one son **Gɛndow**. He died during the Japanese Invasion of Malaya, and his grave can be found at **Taŋkơl P'rawas**, where he had lived.

P'rawas Hill, the home of Taaᵏ K'rundoŋ and his son Taaᵏ Tukaŋ.

The Kalɨᵏ River, at Tagat.

The j'lax tree at Cakob, into which an old woman, Jaaᵏ Cakob, crawled and died.

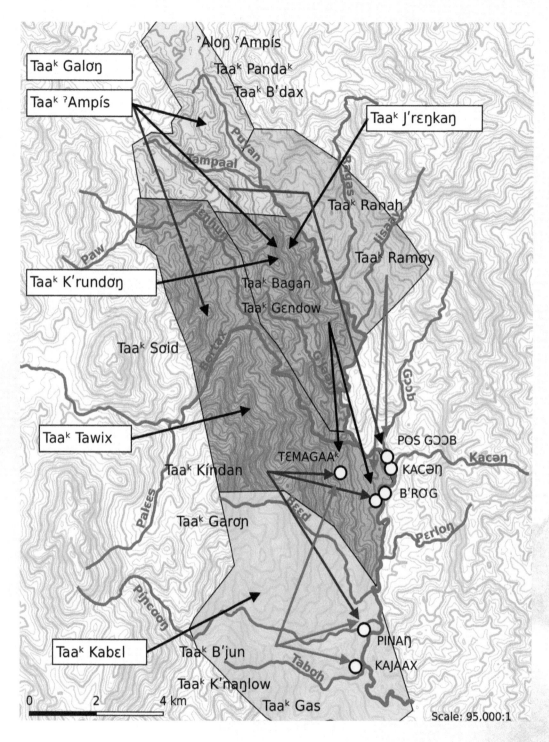

Fig. 5. Map showing the origins of present-day inhabitants of the Pos Gɔɔb villages (excluding the Lower Puyan Temiars). The shaded areas show the possible extent of former dwellings or swiddens, but not hunting or foraging grounds, of their descendants. The earliest ancestors are those names which are boxed on the outside of the map.

7.1.3 Tɛmagaaᵏ: ˀAmpís Galoŋ

Taaᵏ ˀAmpís Galoŋ lived at **Manuŋ** and **Saɲyal**, on the ridge bordering the Bərtax and Puyan Rivers. He is also known to have cut the earliest swiddens in the upper reaches of the Puyan River, at **Gɛjgííjwɛɛd**, on the hill above a tributary river named the **Tampaal**. This was only a few hours walk northward from his home at Saɲyal, along the ridge that leads to K'jay Mountain and the Perak border, and turning at Ŋulŋaal Hill, eastward, down toward **P'cơh** on the Tampaal River.

A Temiar climbs up Bayas Waterfall, on the Puyan River. (Credit: Yusman ˀAndoᵏ)

He had five daughters, **ˀAbơơŋ**, **ˀAsuh**, **Sɛnayih**, **T'míír** and **Cabɛŋ**, and four sons, **ˀAloŋ**, **Roman**, **Laŋsah** and **Bakơh**.

Taaᵏ ˀAmpís was a reknowned Tataaᵏ Bɛlyan, a great soul-medium, and he is revered even until today. He followed his tiger-*guníg* in dreams and saw many of the souls of nature inhabiting the forest and mountains. In one of his dreams a soul of the land took him to the main river and said to him, *"Rantơw Puyan,"* the river and land of the Puyan, that was created by Nyʉᵏ ˀAlʉj, to give life, and from here he would find *bɛlyan* power.

He is otherwise known by the name of Taaᵏ Jaan, because he had a *guníg tawaag*, a butterfly dream guide, that flapped its wings, making a *jaan-jaan* sound. In a dream he saw a great tiger up on the highest mountain of the region, peering over the valleys below. Thus he named the mountain, Jɛlmơl P'naŋơw (as *paŋơw* means to lean on the hand and peer). In keeping with Temiar tradition, he also named his son after this mountain, and that is the reason ˀAlơŋ ˀAmpís is also known as Taaᵏ P'naŋơw. The mountain is also known as Camaah (which possibly comes from the word *c'maas*, steam) and this was the name the British topography surveyors took for the mountain, naming it Gunung Chamah.

His daughter, **ˀAsuh ˀAmpís** was killed, tragically, when a tiger attacked her at the Jɛŋhuŋ River, as she went to wash in the morning. It is said that she broke a taboo (the prohibition called *pɛlˀax*) and brought this misfortune upon herself. Until today, they do not go near that place on the Jɛŋhuŋ (pictured, Vol. 1, p12), as it is feared that a powerful evil presence still haunts there.

Sɛnayih **ʔAmpís** was married to Pandaᵏ, who came to the Puyan from the S'ŋaaᵏ River in Perak (see 7.2 Kampuŋ Pos Gɔɔb). She was brutally murdered by Chinese bandits in the jungle. Her remains were buried on a hill at **Taməŋ**. The bandits caused some anxiety among the Temiars, after they said they were coming to find them and kill them all, so they took their beloved old Taaᵏ ʔAmpís across to **Hariyuw** (later called Tapɛy), on the foothills of Mount Soʼid, to hide him there.

In his late years, Taaᵏ ʔAmpís' returned to **Saɲyal**, at the source of the G'ləəŋ River, and there he died, a venerable and wise Temiar, who is revered until today. His resting place is found nearby on

Taŋkoʼl Ranal. *Tataaᵏ Bɛlyans* were always laid to rest in a burial hut near where they ended their life. The year of his death was possibly around 1950, as the late Pəŋhuluᵏ P'diᵏ K'lusar (born in 1940) remembered he was a young lad of about 10 years at the time and it was also before the *P'raŋ Laɲoʼoy*, the 'war' of the Communists.

The site of Taaᵏ ʔAmpís' home at Saɲyal, where he was also laid to rest, is revered by the Temiars because of their ancestor's status as a powerful halaaᵏ, and they make petitions when they come here, to excuse their presence.

7.1.4   Tɛmagaaᵏ: ʔAloʼŋ ʔAmpís

ʔAloʼŋ ʔAmpís (who is also known as **Taaᵏ P'naŋoʼw**) lived mainly in the upper Puyan tributary valleys, at **Ranah**, **P'coʼh**, **Gɛrhaar**, **J'roʼx**, **Jaŋrax**, and **Bagan**, shifting between the places which his father, Taaᵏ ʔAmpís, had originally inhabited. He cut new plantations there and visited at good hunting or fishing grounds.

He had two daughters, **Tampaal** and **ʔAwɛl**, and four sons, **ʔIsɛɛh**, **K'lusar**, **Muríb** and **ʔAnjaŋ**. He died before his father and his grave is found near **Lawaar**. Some people say that he was murdered by another man, after he refused to share his tobacco with him. The late Pəŋhuluᵏ P'diᵏ couldn't verify this story about his grandfather's death, but perhaps the story had been hushed or, otherwise, it may not be true at all.

Tampaal P'naŋoʼw married and moved to B'tʉs (Kuala Betis), and **ʔAwɛl** to **Pɛrlaᵏ** (which is now named Pulat).

ʔIsɛɛh P'naŋoʼw had one daughter, **ʔAmɛᵏ** (who died at Gombak from TB), and two sons, **ʔAnjaŋ** (died at Tɛmagaaᵏ) and **ʔAdiᵏ** (died in Perak). Both his sons were in the Senoi Praaq, the commando unit manned by Orang Asli soldiers. He died during the stay at Jɛnɛɛs, and was laid to rest at the **Taboʼh** River, along with his wife below today's Kajaax village.

K'lusar P'naŋoʹw lived in the area of the **Lagoh**, **Soʹid** and **Jɛŋhuŋ** Rivers, cutting swiddens and building long-houses at **Lawaar**, **Tapɛy**, **Cɛŋkaar**, **Biraax**, **Sʹʔɛɛb**, **Saɲɛɛn**, **Sʹlipɔɔh**, **Maníᵏ**, **Labuᵏ**, **Bʹrunih**, **Paax** and **Katuᵏ**. He went hunting at **Sajaaᵏ** and up the **Jɛŋhuŋ** River, at **Soh** on the Bərtax-Puyan boundary, on **Soʹid** mountain and westward at the **Palɛɛs** River, following where his forefathers had been, who had passed on the knowledge of the land to him. He planted manioc at Lawaar, but it would not grow because of the soil and so they lived mostly on the meat of game they hunted. Manioc grew well at Lʹbíír and Sʹlipɔɔh. He died in 1977 and his grave is found at **Lawaar**.

The site of Biraax, an old dwelling on the central ridge.

A great tree stump at Saɲɛɛn, an old swidden on Soʹid Mountain.

The old swidden at Sʹlipɔɔh, south of the Bərtax River.

He had three daughters, **ʔabơơŋ**, **C'rɛdhiid** and **ʔAmít**, and two sons, **ʔAlơŋ**, the eldest, and **P'diᵏ**, the third child (the late Penghulu of Tɛmagaaᵏ). ʔAbơơŋ's and ʔAlơŋ's graves are found below Tɛmagaaᵏ. ʔAmít's grave can be found by the roadside, not far from Tɛmagaaᵏ, and was nearly bulldozed away while the logging road was made. C'rɛdhiid's grave is found across the river at Stool.

Muríb P'naŋơw lived with his brother K'lusar, at Lɛŋraaŋ, after the return. He had one son, **ʔAŋah**, who died at Lɛŋraaŋ after he was apparently poisoned at school in Gəmbalah. Muríb died at Lɛŋraaŋ.

ʔAnjaŋ P'naŋơw lived at **K'caaw**, **Tɛmagaaᵏ** and **K'síj**. He had two daughters, **ʔAbơơŋ** and **ʔAsuh**, and four sons, **ʔAbaaŋ** (living at Gawíín), **ʔAŋah**, **Pandaᵏ** and **ʔAdiᵏ** (all died in Perak). He died at Hɛrwɛᵏ, near Jɛnɛɛs, at the time they returned from downriver.

According to Pəŋhuluᵏ P'diᵏ, Taaᵏ K'lusar died in the year 1977. That means we can estimate his year of birth to be **1887**, taken that his age was possibly 90 years old at his death, as Pəŋhuluᵏ P'diᵏ recalls his father as an aged man. Then, if all Pəŋhuluᵏ P'diᵏ's forefathers begot sons at an age of 20-30, then from K'lusar's year of birth we can count back for each forefather, and arrive at their possible years of birth. Those being between **1857** and **1867** for Taaᵏ P'naŋơw, between **1827** and **1847** for Taaᵏ ʔAmpís and between **1797** and **1827** for Taaᵏ Galoŋ. But this is an approximation and there are no written records.

This could mean that Taaᵏ Galoŋ migrated to the area as far back as 1840, or certainly by the year 1880, assuming that he was an experienced hunter at the time (aged at least 40).

7.1.5 Tɛmagaaᵏ: Gɛndow K'rundơŋ

Taaᵏ Gɛndow K'rundơŋ, dwelt in the land of the Puyan. His area of roaming and hunting was in the land west of the Puyan, from the **Kɛnsɛɛy** River (found between the Bərtax and G'ləəŋ Rivers) to the **K'nɛgwɛɛg**, near the **Tampaal**, on the higher Puyan.

He was attacked by a tiger and killed at ˀAmpar ˀƐij. His son, ˀAloʼŋ, and daughter, ˀAndaᵏ, escaped after they managed to run down the valley to safety. But in her tiredness, ˀAndaᵏ had to leave her younger sister, ˀAsuh, on the path and so she was also eaten by the tiger.

Pandoʼᵏ Gɛndow (who is also called ˀAloʼŋ) hunted at the Gʼləəŋ River, planted at Capɛɛr, at the Ragas river-mouth, and roamed up to the Kʼnɛgwɛg River in his father's territory, but he lived with Pəŋhuluᵏ Pʼdiᵏ at Lɛŋraaŋ. He planted durian trees at Kɛntoʼb and cut a plantation at Jʼwaaŋ, near the Kɛnsɛɛy River. He had seven children: two daughters, ˀAboʼoŋ (living at Bərcaap) and ˀAmɛᵏ (moved to Perak), and five sons, ˀAnjaŋ (died in Perak), ˀAli, ˀAziz (both moved to Perak), ˀAŋah (living at Tɛmagaaᵏ) and ˀAdiᵏ (living at Bərcaap). His grave is found at Gʼləəŋ.

7.1.6   Tɛmagaaᵏ: Taaᵏ Tawix

Taaᵏ Tawix moved to the area in the time of Taaᵏ ˀAmpís, from Gerik in Perak. His son was Taaᵏ Kíndan. They lived at Sʼrijoʼoʼh, on the Bərtax River. Kíndan had four daughters, ˀAtih (also called Pʼgoʼy because she was born at the mountain pass near Mount Pʼgoʼy), ˀAboʼoŋ (died at Jɛnɛɛs), ˀAndaᵏ (moved to Pasíg) and ˀAsuh (the late first wife of Pəŋhuluᵏ Pʼdiᵏ, died at Sapɛd), and two sons, Bʼloʼy and Bərlɛy. He died from a disease caused by the bərboʼw, or ironwood tree, which is feared to contain an evil soul in Temiar custom and carries taboos. He was buried at Tanjuŋ, across the Puyan from Gʼləəŋ, on the east bank.

His two sons lived at Sʼrijoʼoʼh, but during the instability of the Communist era, they moved away from the Bərtax to the Píncoʼoŋ River, where their descendants can be found living today at Pinaŋ and Tanjuŋ villages.

Bʼloʼy Kíndan, the eldest son, had six children: two daughters, ˀAbaaɲ (Pəŋhuluᵏ Pʼdiᵏ's second wife, died at Tɛmagaaᵏ) and ˀAboʼoŋ (died young), and four sons, ˀAbus (died young), ˀAŋah, ˀUda (both died in Perak) and Milor (died young). Taaᵏ Bʼloʼy moved to Gerik after the return from the resettlement, and he died there.

ˀAtih Kíndan was married to Sisam, who came from Perak, and they had seven children: three daughters, ˀAboʼoŋ (died at Sʼrijoʼoʼh), ˀAndoʼᵏ (died at Bʼroʼg) and Hɛnərix (the late first wife of Pəŋhuluᵏ ˀUsop, of Pinaŋ), and four sons, ˀAlaŋ (died at Pʼlad), ˀAbus (living at Pinaŋ), ˀAŋah (died at Gombak), and ˀAlʉj (living at Pinaŋ). ˀAtih died and was buried near Pɛrloʼŋ.

Hɛnərix trod on something poisonous in a pool at Pʼlad, soon after she had given birth to her youngest child. They say it was a ndaŋgaaᵏ (the subterranean serpent) that bit her foot and that she shouldn't have gone out so soon after child-birth, when the smell was still strong on her. Due to the 'bite' her body swelled up and she died.

Bərlɛy Kíndan had three sons, ˀAŋah (moved to Pos Kimaar), ˀAhíŋ (died at Pinaŋ) and ˀAyob (living at Tanjuŋ). Taaᵏ Bərlɛy lived at Kampuŋ Jʼrɛntaaŋ, with the Kɛnrɛn Temiars after the return, and he died there. His body was taken down-river by raft and laid to rest in a burial hut at the Lɛmpar river-mouth.

7.1.7 Tɛmagaaᵏ: Gəslas Mɛndol

Gəslas Mɛndol (or **Lunaŋ**), born in Perak, was a contemporary of Taaᵏ K′lusar, and is otherwise known as **Taaᵏ Soʼid** because he died of hunger on Mount Soʼid while walking back from R′koʼob. He lived in the Upper Bərtax region with the K′lusar clan. He had one daughter, **Samiᵏ** (living at Goʼob), and three sons, **ʔAloʼŋ** (died at Tɛmagaaᵏ), **ʔAnjaŋ** (living at Tɛmagaaᵏ) and **Mɛbɔʼᵏ** (moved to Bidor).

Taaᵏ Lunaŋ (father of Gɛslas) had a contemporary named **Taaᵏ Wawoh** (probably his brother), whose son was **ʔAlʉj**, and grandson was **Punɛy**.

7.1.8 Tɛmagaaᵏ: Taaᵏ Garoɲ

Taaᵏ Garoɲ was a Lanoh from Ciyuŋ, in Perak. His two sons came to the Puyan and they were **Sagər** and **Sɛdlíj**. They both lived at **B′rawɛɛɲ**, in the 1970s, at the Puyan river-side, but moved back to Perak later.

Sagər Garoɲ had four daughters, **Luntin**, **ʔAtiw**, **Bitul** (all three moved to Ciyuŋ) and **ʔAsuh** (living at Tɛmagaaᵏ), and one son, **Raŋgɛl**. He died at Ciyuŋ.

Sɛdlij Garoɲ had three sons, **ʔAɲah** (living at Tɛmagaaᵏ), **ʔAdən** and **Pandoʼᵏ** (both died in Perak).

Taaᵏ Rɛgbag was another Lanoh from Perak. His son was **Tuŋgal**. Tuŋgal had a daughter, **ʔAmɛᵏ** (living at Bərcaap), and a son **ʔItam**. ʔItam had one son, **ʔAbaaɲ**. Both Tuŋgal and ʔItam died and were buried at **Sapɛd**, in the tip of land between the Bərtax and the Puyan Rivers.

ʔAbaaɲ ʔItam was married to S′ritah Ramoʼy of the Puyan Temiars and lived at Pos Goʼob until his death.

7.1.9 Tɛmagaaᵏ: Taaᵏ J′rɛŋkaŋ

Taaᵏ J′rɛŋkaŋ came from the **Yaay** River, south of the Pɛriyas. He had one daughter, **Bacap**, and two sons, **ʔOrɛᵏ** and **T′wal**. He lived with his sons at **Soh**, on the ridge between the Bərtax and Puyan River valleys.

ʔOrɛᵏ J′rɛŋkaŋ had one son **ʔAlʉj**.

ʔAlʉj had four sons, **Saga**, **ʔAɲah** (both moved to Perak), **Norman** (living at Tɛmagaaᵏ) and **Busu** (living at B′roʼg). He was born at **Luwag Naŋkaaᵏ**, the gully where a jack-fruit tree grew of itself, not far from Soh.

T′wal J′rɛŋkaŋ had one son **Ɖah**, who lived at **Bagan**, a hill named after a large jungle durian tree there, and so he was also known as **Taaᵏ Bagan**. Ɖah had two daughters, **ʔƏniriŋ** (died at Goʼob) and **ʔAmɛᵏ** (living at Goʼob), and two sons, **ʔAdiᵏ** (died at Goʼob) and **ʔAlʉj** (living at Goʼob). He died and was buried at **Taŋkoʼl Bagan**.

Taaᵏ Kᶜlusar
26. Lawaar, 27. Cenkaar,
28. Biraax, 29. Sajaaᵏ,
30. Sᶜɛɛb, 31. Soh,
32. Tapɛɛy, 33. Lᶜbiir,
34. Sᶜnun, 35. Layan,
36. Paax, 37. Katuᵏ,
38. Labuᵏ, 39. Cɛrpoor,
40. Sᶜlipɔɔh, 41. Maniᵏ,
42. Sanɛɛn.

Taaᵏ Kᶜrundon
10. Tagat, 11. Calyɛx,
12. Sᶜtool, 13. Pᶜrawas.

Taaᵏ Rewrow
20. Rewroow,
21. ᶜEntɛɛb,
22. Jɛrhoh.

Taaᵏ ᶜAmpis
23. Bᶜrunih,
24. Sanyal,
25. Manun,
p1. Gɛjgiijwɛɛd,
p2. Janrax,
p3. Bagan.

Taaᵏ Galon
1. Tajɔɔr,
2. Kalan,
3. Sigan,
4. Tᶜlor,
5. Sᶜrijooth,
6. Sᶜpooy,
7. Siyaduh,
8. Papan,
9. Temagaaᵏ.

Taaᵏ Kᶜcaaw
14. Kᶜcaaw, 15. Pakuᵏ,
16. Kᶜmooᵏ, 17. Cakob,
18. Tayug, 19. Tᶜramoᵏ.

Fig. 6. Map showing the pre-1950s dwellings of the Bərtax River Temiars. The caves where people sought refuge are shown as dark spots, and several bomb craters from the 1954 RAF bombing are shown as red spots (see Chapter 8). The dashed green lines demarcate the boundary between the the sakaaᵏ of the different Temiar kin groups. The dotted brown lines shows the main ancient paths that traverse the land between the long-houses, reaching up to the boundaries with Perak and the neighbouring Temiar territories.

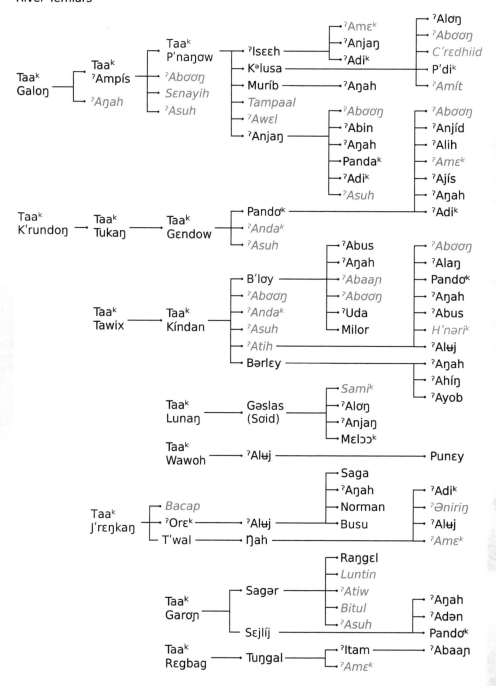

Fig. 7. Ancestry of the Bərtax River Temiars, living at today's Tɛmagaaᵏ, Bərcaap, Pinaŋ and Tanjuŋ villages. Names in black indicate males, names in green, females. The names of the last generation in the tree represent the grandfathers and grandmothers of today, although not all are still living. The names of all their children might add up to another hundred or more.

7.2 KAMPUŊ POS GƆƆB

The original homeland of the Temiars of present-day Pos Gɔɔb, Kacəŋ, and B'rơg villages, lies at the upper reaches of the Puyan and its tributaries, the Ragas and Tampaal Rivers. Many are descended from Taaᵏ ˀAmpís (see 7.1 Kampuŋ Tɛmagaaᵏ), through his daughter's marriage to Taaᵏ Pandaᵏ (see below), but others from certain Temiars who migrated from Perak.

7.2.1 Gɔɔb: ˀAmpís Galoŋ

It was **Taaᵏ ˀAmpís** who cut the first plantation at the Puyan head-waters, on the hill at **Gɛjgííjwɛɛd**, so named because a man's loin cloth caught fire as he sat to warm himself. Taaᵏ ˀAmpís was the son of **Taaᵏ Galoŋ** who lived on the Bərtax River. In those days the Temiars moved about freely in their land, building a bamboo long-house wherever it was good to plant their yam or millet and camping under temporary shelters wherever the hunting or fishing was best. Taaᵏ ˀAmpís must have found the upper Puyan area to be ideal for planting and also good for hunting game and he cut swiddens at **Jaŋrax**, **P'cơh** and **Bagan**, as well as at the **Talơŋ** River head over the watershed boundary in Perak. He could move freely between the Upper Puyan and Talơŋ Rivers because the path over the boundary was easy, with no steep climbs or mountain peaks and it could be walked over in one morning. The upper river areas are cool, with ample small rivers, and ideal for planting millet and other crops.

The tree stumps of great mahoganies cut down by Taaᵏ ˀAmpís, a hundred years ago, still remain at Gɛjgííjwɛɛd.

Gɛjgɨ́jwɛ̃d

Janɛax

7.2.2   Gɔɔb: Panda^k T'rơŋ

Possibly a hundred years ago, **Panda^k T'rơŋ** migrated from the P'lus River in Perak and made his way over the mountains to B'latim, on the Panɛɛs River. From there he came down to Cabay, and from there he came to the Pɛriyas, and walked north to the Puyan. He was looking for land that he could settle in with enough game to hunt. When he reached the higher Puyan he would have met Taa^k ʔAmpís and his family and, in time, he married Taa^k ʔAmpís' daughter, **Sɛnayih**, and he settled at the P'cơh River, a small tributary of the Tampaal. He made his territory from the **K'nɛgwɛg** as far as the **Talơŋ** in Perak (and thus he was also called Taa^k Talơŋ), including the swiddens of **P'cơh** and **Gɛrhaar**.

He had a daughter, **Lɛ^kŋi^k** (died in Perak), and three sons, **ʔAlaŋ**, **Bơŋsu** and **Tɛŋah** (all three lived and died at Gɔɔb and were buried at **Habog**). ʔAlaŋ and Bơŋsu were the leaders of the Upper Puyan Temiars during the gathering by the British (see Chapter 8), and they were both made Penghulu over the Puyan River region. Taa^k Panda^k died at T'rơŋ, in Perak.

ʔAlaŋ Panda^k had one daughter, **ʔAslím**, and three sons, **Liman**, **ʔUda** and **Jambu** (all living today at Gɔɔb).

ʔAlaŋ and his brother, Tɛŋah, moved about together, also with Pandơ^k Gɛndow, cutting swiddens at places in the Upper Puyan area, where their fathers, ʔAlơŋ ʔAmpís and Gɛndow Tukaŋ had lived before them. These places included **P'cơh**, **Tamaŋ**, **Tandiŋ**, **Canaŋ**, **Lapơg**, **C'naap**, **Cəlʔɛl**, **Karas**, **Sayơơj**, **S'mɛɛy**, **Pacɛy**, **Bagan**, **Kɛntɛb**, **Pulɛy**, **Mata^k**, **ʔIlōn^k**, and **Capɛɛr**.

The old swidden of Gɛrhaar.

The old dwelling of P'coh, which later became an army landing point, called Poŋ Brabo.

Tree stumps at K'míɲam, the old swidden they cut while living at Canaŋ.

At **Jaŋrax**, the old dwelling of their grandfather, Taa^k ²Ampís, they lived together with their brother Bơŋsu and ²Alơŋ Ramơy. Taa^k B′dax and Siyam P′hεεɲ joined them at **P′cơh**, while Taa^k T′wal lived at **Bagan**.

Bơŋsu Panda^k had one daughter, **²Abɔɔ^k**, and three sons, **²Alơŋ** (who died at Gerik after being poisoned at a tea shop), **²Aŋah** (died at Gɔɔb) and **²Asơd** (living at B′rơg). He was known as the last Tataa^k Bεlyan in the region and he knew *halaa^k*. He also had dealings with the Communists, such as negotiating with them to surrender themselves to the government.

Bơŋsu moved about with ²Alơŋ Ramơy and ²Anjaŋ Buŋaa^k, cutting swiddens in places to the east of the Puyan River, in the same valleys where their fathers, Taa^k Ramơy and Taa^k Buŋaa^k, had lived before them. These places included, **Lεrləər**, **Ranah**, **R′sεεm**, **Tapεl**, **Gεrhaar**, **J′rơx**, **S′lεmnam**, **Papan**, **Kalaŋ**, **Rεnipuy**, **S′raŋε^k** (where quartz fire stones could be found in the river), **Ragas**, **²Ayơy**, **Maŋgəs**, **B′kah** and **Siruy**.

When the groups of Temiars were gathered from around the Puyan, Boŋsu and Ramóy may have been living at Lɛrləər at the time, and thus Ranah, a three-minute walk away, would have been chosen as the most ideal site for a landing zone. Boŋsu was called by a new name by the British, whatever it was, and it stuck as Hɛlwəd. Hence this former penghulu is always referred to as Boŋsu Hɛlwəd, rather than Boŋsu Panda[k].

ta[k]

Maŋgəs

B'kah

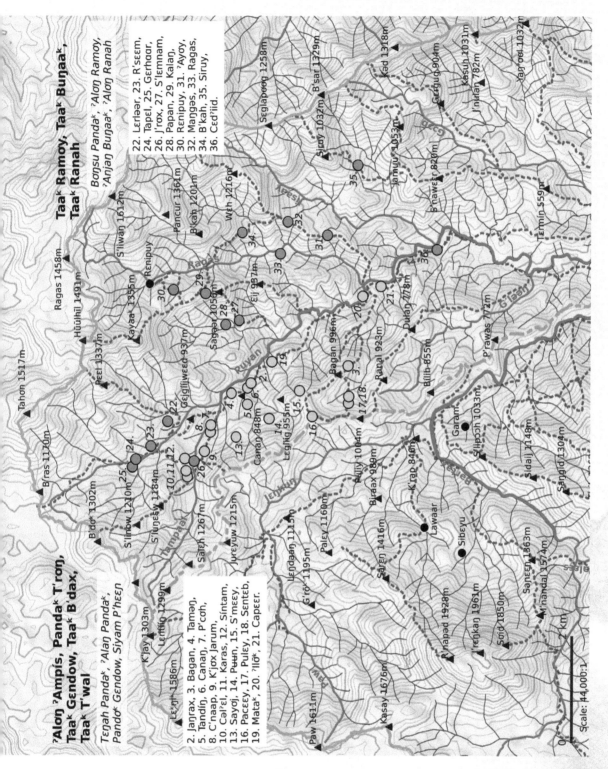

Fig. 8. Map showing the pre-1950s dwellings of the Puyan River Temiars. The caves where people sought refuge are shown as dark spots.

7.2.3 Gɔɔb: Taaᵏ Ramoʾy

Taaᵏ Ramoʾy was from R'kooʾb . He lived at **Manuŋ**, on the Bərtax-Puyan boundary, in the time of Taaᵏ K'lusar. He also hunted in the Jisay River area, east of the Puyan, and cut a swidden at Siruy. He had two sons, **ʔAloʾŋ** and **ʔItam**, and one daughter, **S'ritah**. His grave is found at Gɔɔb.

ʔAloʾŋ Ramoʾy lived at **Maŋgəs**, **B'kah**, **S'lɛmnam**, **Papan**, **R'sɛɛm** and **Lɛrləər**, on the east side of the Puyan, together with Boʾŋsu Pandaᵏ. He had two sons, **Jusni** and **ʔUda** (both retired from the Army and living at Bərcaap). He was also known as Taaᵏ Sakol because of his white hair. He died at Gɔɔb.

ʔItam Ramoʾy had six children: two daughters, **ʔAbooʾŋ** (died at Ipoh) and Horiyon (moved to Pos Kimaar in Perak), and four sons, **ʔAnjaŋ** (died at Gombak), **ʔAdiᵏ** (living at Bərcaap), **ʔAlaŋ** (died at Gɔɔb) and **ʔAsoʾd** (died at Bayuur, Pos Pasíg). He died at the S'ŋaaᵏ River, Perak.

S'ritah Ramoʾy lives at B'roʾg. She married **ʔAbaaɲ ʔItam** (son of ʔItam Tuŋgal) and they had nine children: five daughters, **K'sal** and **ʔAndaᵏ** (both living at B'roʾg), **ʔAɲah** (died at Kacəŋ, wife of the late ʔUda Siyam), **ʔAbooʾŋ** (died at Tɛmagaaᵏ), and **ʔAtih** (living at B'roʾg), and four sons, **ʔɛmbah** (died at Gɔɔb), **ʔAziz**, **Sadəri**, and **Rɛni** (all living at B'roʾg).

A Temiar hikes up a ridge from the Jisay River valley, towards the boundary with Bayuur.

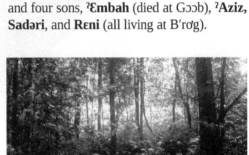

Siruy

7.2.4 Gɔɔb: Taaᵏ Ranah

Taaᵏ Ranah lived at **Maŋgəs**. His son was **ʔAloʾŋ**, who was known as 'Taaᵏ Pooʾs' because his short pants were ragged and looked like the leaves of an *ʔapooʾs* (zingiber) plant.

ʔAloʾŋ Ranah had eight children: four daughters, **ʔAhoʾy** (living at Gɔɔb), **ʔAbooʾŋ**, **Rimbon** and **Lurah** (all three moved to Pasíg), and four sons, **Kɛntoʾn** (living at Bərcaap, retired from the Army), **Barín** (moved to Yaay), **ʔAli** and **Rasíp** (both moved to Pasíg). ʔAbooʾŋ was called "Tihaŋ", to describe her large nostrils.

7.2.5 Gɔɔb: Taaᵏ B'dax

Taaᵏ B'dax came from the **C'nɛnduŋ River**, at **Ciyuŋ** in Perak. His son was **Cɛrlóy**, and he lived at **B'raboh**, then called **P'cóh**, on the **Tampaal** River (the name B'raboh comes from the time of the Senoi Praaq, who opened the site for an Army landing zone, which presumably they called Point Bravo).

Cɛrlóy B'dax had a daughter, **ʔAmɛᵏ**, and three sons, **ʔAlóŋ**, **ʔAdiᵏ** and **ʔAlʉj**. ʔAdiᵏ moved to Ciyuŋ, but the other three live at **Cadóoɲ**, at Pos Gɔɔb. Cɛrlóy died at the **Sɛŋsiŋ** River.

7.2.6 Gɔɔb: Taaᵏ P'hɛɛɲ

Taaᵏ P'hɛɛɲ was from **ʔUyas**, on the B'róóx River, and Gəmbalah, on the Jɛnrol. He moved to the Upper Puyan before the relocation that began in 1954, and lived at **P'cóh**. He also cut swiddens over the border at the Upper S'ŋaaᵏ in Perak. He had two sons, **Siyam**, who continued living at the Puyan River, and **ʔAɲah**, who returned to B'riix, at the Jɛnról.

Siyam P'hɛɛɲ had seven children: two daughters, **Mah** (died at Gɔɔb) and **ʔAndaᵏ** (moved to Kimaar), and five sons, **ʔUda** (died at Kacəŋ), **Nor ʔApat** (died in Perak), **Saidi** (living at Cabay), **Miyor** and **ʔAsnan** (both living at Pos Pasíg).

ʔUda was born at the **Taloŋ** River in Perak and through his father he knew all the swiddens of the Upper Puyan and of the river sources over in Perak. He was recruited into the Senoi Praaq, and once gave important information that led to a commando operation on a terrorist jungle camp.

ʔAɲah P'hɛɛɲ, who lived at B'riix, married at the **Píɲcóóŋ** River and had five children: two daughters, **Jadɛɛr** (died in Perak), **ʔAnor** (living at Pos Piyəh in Perak), and three sons, **Kudín** (living at Tɛmagaaᵏ), **Roslan** (living at Pinaŋ) and **Jaᵏpar** (living in Perak). He lives today at Pinaŋ, one of the oldest still living at the Puyan.

7.2.7 Gɔɔb: Taaᵏ ʔAwih

Taaᵏ ʔAwih was from the **Lɛmpaar** River, in the Pɛriyas valley, and he lived at the **K'ləəd River**. His son **ʔAti** came up-river to the Puyan River source at the time of Pandaᵏ T'roŋ, and lived with his family. ʔAti had two sons, **ʔAndóᵏ** and **ʔAlʉj**. ʔAndóᵏ was a soldier in the Home Guard, and he died at B'róg.

7.2.8 Gɔɔb: Taaᵏ Buŋaaᵏ

Taaᵏ Buŋaaᵏ lived at the same time as Taaᵏ Pandaᵏ, at the **Lɛrləər** and the **R'sɛɛm** Rivers. One of his sons, **ʔAnjaŋ**, lived at **S'lɛmnam**, before migrating away to the Pasíg area, where his descendants are found today.

Ancestry of the Upper Puyan River Temiars

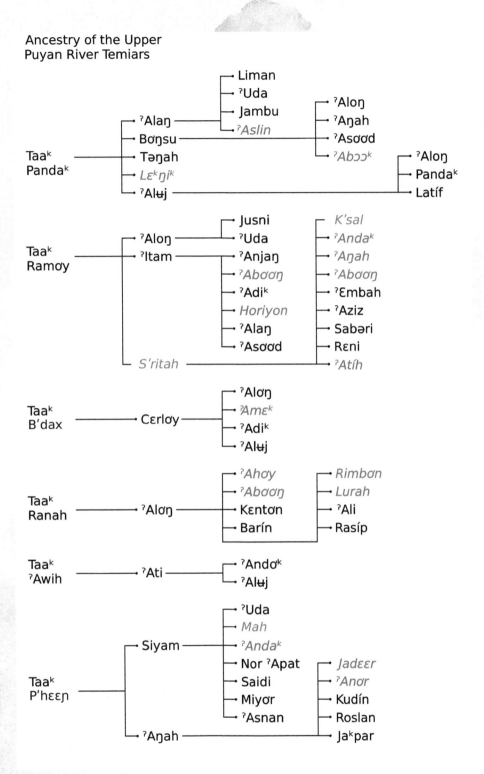

Fig. 9. Ancestry of the Upper Puyan River Temiars, living today at Pos Gɔɔb, B'rơg, Bərcaap and Pinaŋ villages.

7.3   KAMPUꟿ PINAꟿ

The furthest known ancestors of the Temiars living today at Pinaŋ village (and also at Kajaax village, until 2019), are **Taaᵏ Kabɛl**, **Taaᵏ B'jun**, **Taaᵏ K'naŋlow** and **Taaᵏ Gas**, all of whom lived around a hundred years ago. Some at Pinaŋ today are descended from these four ancestors but others have moved here from the Bərtax clan (descendants of **B'lơy Kíndan** and **Bərlɛy Kíndan**) and from down the valley, such as from Pos Pasíg and Jadɛɛr village at Pos Símpor.

7.3.1   Pinaŋ: Taaᵏ Kabɛl

Taaᵏ Kabɛl lived at **Kayaaᵏ**, on the Píɲcơơŋ River, in the years of peace and he had one son, **ˀAti**. He shifted and planted up and down the river, as there were ample small rivers, fruit trees, and wild animals to hunt. He made hunting camps at **Gooc**, **Ləruw**, **T'ŋơᵏ** and **Jasaar**, which were sited high on the river, in the vicinity of the spectacular Ləruw waterfall. He also planted swiddens at **ˀOwɨŋ**, **Hơơb**, **Jɛrsɛɛp** and **C'rɛɛy**. Whenever he wanted to fish at the main river he would stay at **Pinaŋ**, which was situated near the Píɲcơơŋ river-mouth. He died in a cave at the Píɲcơơŋ River, that is now named after him, Guwɔɔᵏ Kabɛl. He was a Tataaᵏ Bɛlyan and he kept a tiger *guníg*.

ˀAti Kabɛl had five children, of which only the youngest is alive today: **ˀAbơơŋ** (who died at Tohơy), ˀUsop (the late Penghulu of Pinaŋ), **S'man** (died at Pasíg), **Sɛnjon** (died in Perak), and ˀAsuh (married to ˀAbus Sisam). ˀAti died at P'lad, and was laid to rest there on the hill, near the Puyan River. He also had been a great soul medium and kept a tiger *guníg*, even as his father had done.

The forest at Kayaaᵏ, the oldest settlement of the Píɲcơơŋ Temiars.
(Credit for Píɲcơơŋ pictures: Rapi)

A cave at T'ŋoʻoᵏ, used by hunters.

A hunting camp at Gooc.

Jasar waterfall, at Jasar.

Sɛmpaaᵏ Kabɛl, the jungle durian tree of Taaᵏ Kabɛl, at ʔOwiŋ.

7.3.2   Pinaŋ: Taaᵏ B′jun

Taaᵏ B′jun lived at **Labuᵏ** and **Bagan** and had four children: two daughters, **ʔAbơơŋ** and **T′gɛw** (who both died while young, from the sickness at Jɛnɛɛs), and three sons, **R′masa**, **Harơd** (called **J′muloᵏ**), and **Mudah**. He made swiddens at **Sumbaah**, **Lɛrwɛɛr** and **S′maliyɛx**, and he also made a dwelling at **Bɛɛd**, on the Puyan. He often went down-river to stay at the **Jɛnrơl** because the fish were plentiful in that day. He died there at the Jɛnrơl.

R′masa B′jun lived at **Labuᵏ** and **Bagan**, and also over the ridge from there at the **B′laʔəər** River. He married Taaᵏ K′naŋlow's daughter, **Hawah**, and had two sons, **ʔAnjaŋ** (who migrated south to Bəər) and **ʔAdiᵏ** (died at Pinaŋ), and one daughter, **S′rɛdʔud** (who moved to Perak). Hawah also had another son, **Raŋɛᵏ** (died at B′riix), and a daughter, **Kowɛᵏ**, by R′masa's nephew, Pandoᵏ Harơd. Taaᵏ R′masa also died at the Jɛnrơl, while his son, ʔAdiᵏ, was still an infant. ʔAdiᵏ lived at **S′maliyɛx**, on the Tabơh River, all his life, but moved to Pinaŋ later because of the elephants.

ʔAbơơŋ B′jun married **Taaᵏ Labuᵏ,** and had two daughters, **Bɔɔᵏ Loŋ** (who died giving birth) and **ʔAndaᵏ** (who died at Canul at the B′laʔəər River), and a son, **Busu** (died at Kajaax, in 2019).

Harơd B′jun fell from a high *k′jơx* tree at the Canul River, while gumming birds, and he died from severe wounds.

T′gɛw B′jun married Taaᵏ K′naŋlow's son, **Padín**.

A contemporary of Taaᵏ B′jun was **Taaᵏ Cɛnwah** (whose father's name is not remembered) and he lived at Bɛɛd, not far from the old Pinaŋ, on the Puyan River. He had seven children; four daughters, one of whom was **ʔAŋah**, and three sons, **ʔAnjaŋ**, **Pərdih** and **ʔAlʉj** (also called Galɛɛr). All of them moved to Pasíg except for Pərdih.

Pərdih Cɛnwah remained a bachelor. He became Penghulu at Pinaŋ after Pəŋhuluᵏ Mudah went to Perak and died there. Pərdih was killed when a tree fell on him, while he was cutting a swidden at **Habog**, at the Bɛɛd River.

Sumbaah (Credit: Rapi)

S'maliyɛx

Lɛrwɛɛr

7.3.3   Pinaŋ: Taaᵏ K′naŋlow

Taaᵏ K′naŋlow lived at the **Taboʰ** and was a cousin of Taaᵏ B′jun. He had three children, a daughter, **Hawah**, and two sons, **Padín** and **Mudah**. His grave can be found near the *jiyɛɛs* tree at Taboʰ.

Taaᵏ Padín lived at Labuᵏ. He had five daughters, **Guwaŋ**, **ʔAndaᵏ**, **ʔAmɛᵏ**, **ʔOrɛh** and **ʔAsuh**, and two sons, **Pandoʼᵏ** (died at Pinaŋ) and **ʔAbus** (who was called Bakaaɲ because he was bitten by a civet).

7.3.4   Pinaŋ: Taaᵏ Gas

Taaᵏ Gas lived at the **B'la²əər River**, by a small tributary called the **P'rəᵏ**. He also made a swidden at **Sumyaŋ**, at the Puyan River. He had four daughters, **Batul**, **²Amow**, **Siríg** and **²Asɛŋ**. Only Batul married.

Batul Gas married **²Aŋah Gɛrbɔɔᵏ** (also known as **Lơwcu**). They had four daughters, **²Andəh**, **Loncat**, **Siyaŋ** and **²Agug**, and one son, **²Abəəh**. ²Andəh had no children, and ²Abəəh and ²Agug died while young. Batul died at Jɛnɛɛs during the return from the displacement, and her grave is with the other graves there—reportedly over 100 of them, as so many died from sickness while living there. ²Aŋah and ²Agug died some years later at **K'maar Hill**, near Lɛŋraaŋ, and were buried there.

Loncat ²Aŋah had one son, **²Aŋah** (who lives at B'riix, Pos Pasíg, today).

Siyaŋ ²Aŋah married ²Aŋah P'hɛɛɲ, who survives her today, living at Pinaŋ village.

A great tree stump still stands at Sumyaŋ, that was cut down with the adze. (Credit: Rapi)

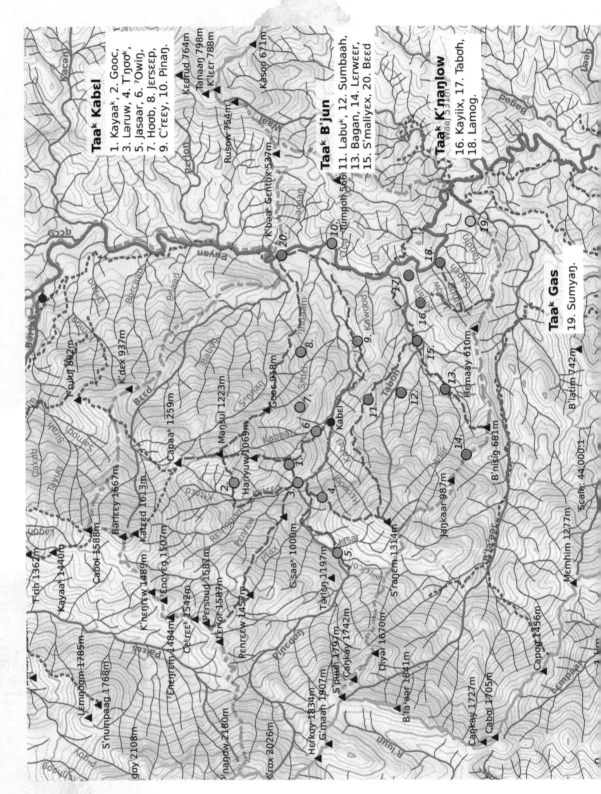

Fig. 10. Map showing the pre-1950s dwellings of the Píncoʼoŋ River Temiars.

Ancestry of the Píɲcɤɤŋ
River Temiars

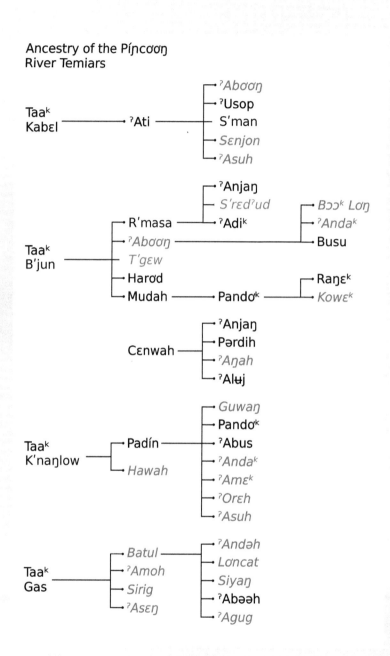

Fig. 11. Ancestry of the Píɲcɤɤŋ River Temiars, living at Pinaŋ (Píɲcɤɤŋ) village.

7.4 KAMPUŊ GAWÍÍN

According to ʔAbaaɲ ʔAnjaŋ, a venerable old man of Kampuŋ Gawíín, and a descendant of Taaᵏ ʔAmpís, many of the Temiars at Gawíín, Calɛɛr and Guwaaɲ villages, which are all on the same hill, are also descended from the same, revered ʔAmpís Galoŋ. Three sons of Taaᵏ ʔAmpís, named, **Roman**, **Laŋsah** and **Bakơh**, lived at the **Lɛrbor** river-mouth on the Lower Puyan. This was the earliest dwelling of the Temiars in this area.

Another prominent ancestor of these Temiars is **Taaᵏ J'raŋkas**, who resided with the sons of ʔAmpís, and his son was **S'magar**.

They dwelt in many other locations all around, wherever it was good for hunting or planting, from **K'maraaᵏ** on the B'laʔəər River, as far as **Kərbaah** on the Lower Puyan River, roaming the land freely. They cut swiddens at places named **B'lukar**, **Sowơj**, **Kəmboŋ**, **M'nakan**, **Rankɛŋ**, **Jaŋwaar**, **Calaag**, **T'ramơᵏ**, **ʔƐndíŋ**, **Kɛjwơơj**, **Batɛŋ**, **Rambɛy**, **Sumbaah**, **K'libooᵏ**, **Sɛrbəər**, **Kɛldơŋ**, **Cɛlcul** and **S'pơơy**.

At the B'laʔəər River they cut swiddens at **Sɛrmaar**, **Tɛŋtɛɛx**, **K'jɛl**, **P'rəᵏ**, **Puŋgəŋ**, **Ríŋud**, **Salơg**, **Nyơy**, **Canul** and **J'riyɛw**. At the Waaj River they planted crops at **Pulɛy** and **T'lambaᵏ**. Some swiddens were made on the boundary of the land also, such as at **Hɛ̄ɛ̄ᵏ** and **Jawaᵏ**, on the boundary with the Pɛriyas valley, and **Luwag Bawaaj**, **Taŋkơl Pantɛy**, and **Taŋkơl Cɛrmɛɛr**, at the boundary with the Bayuur River valley.

Other swiddens were cut further downriver, nearer the mouth of the Puyan, at **J'rɛntaaɲ**, **Malơŋ**, **Pundơŋ** and **Kaləəh**. But these were cut by Temiars from a different ancestry to the Temiars descended from Taaᵏ ʔAmpís.

Lɛrbor

The B'laʔəər River, at K'maraᵏ. (Credit for Lower Puyan pictures: Wahab ʔAlʉj)

K'jɛl

P'rək

Puŋgəŋ

When the so-called *masa lurat* or time of war began, these ancestors, the sons of Taaᵏ ʔAmpís, fled down-river to **Katơᵏ**, and there they stayed until their death.

Roman ʔAmpís had one daughter, **Busuh**, and two sons, **ʔAdiᵏ** and **Kadɛy**.

Kadɛy Roman had two sons, **ʔAlơŋ** and **ʔAnjaŋ**. ʔAlơŋ's son was **ʔOmar**, who moved to Pos Pasíg.

Laŋsah ʔAmpís had one daughter, **ʔAŋah**, and four sons, **ʔAlaŋ**, **ʔAhɛb**, **Caŋkih** and **ʔAlɵj**, who all lived at K'ləəd after the return. ʔAhɛb and ʔAlɵj Laŋsah had no children.

Caŋkih Laŋsah had one daughter, **Gumrəᵏ** (living at Pos Tohơy).

Bakơh ʔAmpís had one son, **Pandaᵏ**, whose two sons were **ʔAlơŋ** and **K'haay**.

K'haay Pandaᵏ was made the second Penghulu of Pos Kɛnrɛn. Pəŋhuluᵏ K'haay had one daughter, **ʔAtih**, and one son, **ʔAlɵj**.

The ancestry of the B'laʔəər River Temiars is by no means as complete as those of the Bərtax, Puyan or Pípcơơŋ Temiars, due to the fact that there are too few persons still surviving who have detailed knowledge of their origins.

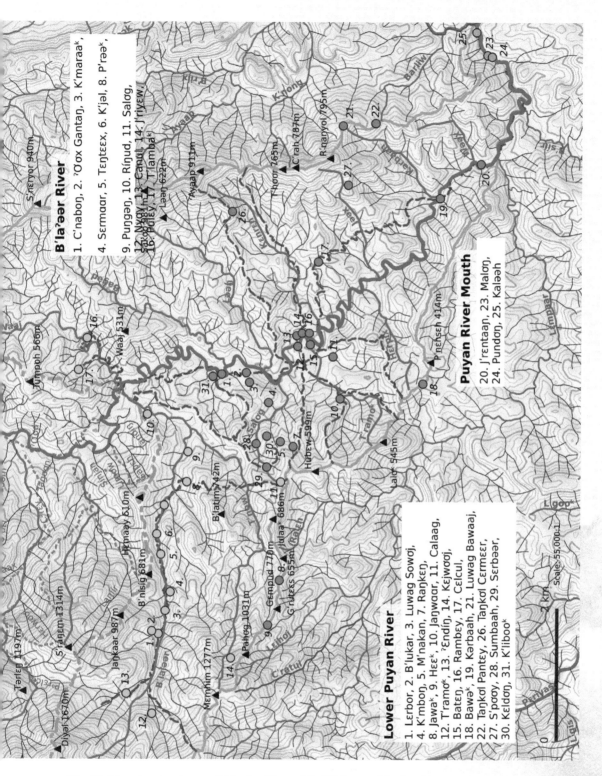

B'laˀəər River

1. C'naboŋ, 2. ˀOox Gantaŋ, 3. K'maraaᵏ,
4. Sɛrmaar, 5. Teŋtɛɛx, 6. K'iǰəl, 8. Pʰraaᵏ,
9. Puŋgəŋ, 10. Riɲud, 11. Salog,
12. Nyɔɔ, 13. Canuul, 14. Jʰriyɛw,
16. Puleɣ, 17. T'lambaᵏ

Puyan River Mouth

20. Jʰrɛntaaŋ, 23. Maloŋ,
24. Pundoŋ, 25. Kaləəh

Lower Puyan River

1. Lɛrbor, 2. B'lukar, 3. Luwag Sowǰ,
4. K'mboŋ, 5. M'nakan, 7. Raŋkɛŋ,
8. Jawaᵏ, 9. Hɛɛᵏ, 10. Jaŋwaar, 11. Calaag,
12. Tʰramoᵏ, 13. ˀɛndiŋ, 14. Kɛjwɔɔǰ,
15. Batɛŋ, 16. Rambɛɣ, 17. Cɛlcul,
18. Bawaᵏ, 19. Kərbaah, 21. Luwag Bawaaǰ,
22. Taŋkəl Pantɛɣ, 26. Taŋkəl Cɛrmɛɛr,
27. S'pooɣ, 28. Sumbaah, 29. Sɛrbəər,
30. Kɛldɔŋ, 31. K'libooᵏ

Fig. 12. Map showing the pre-1950s dwellings of the B'laˀəər and Lɛrbor River Temiars, in the Lower Puyan.

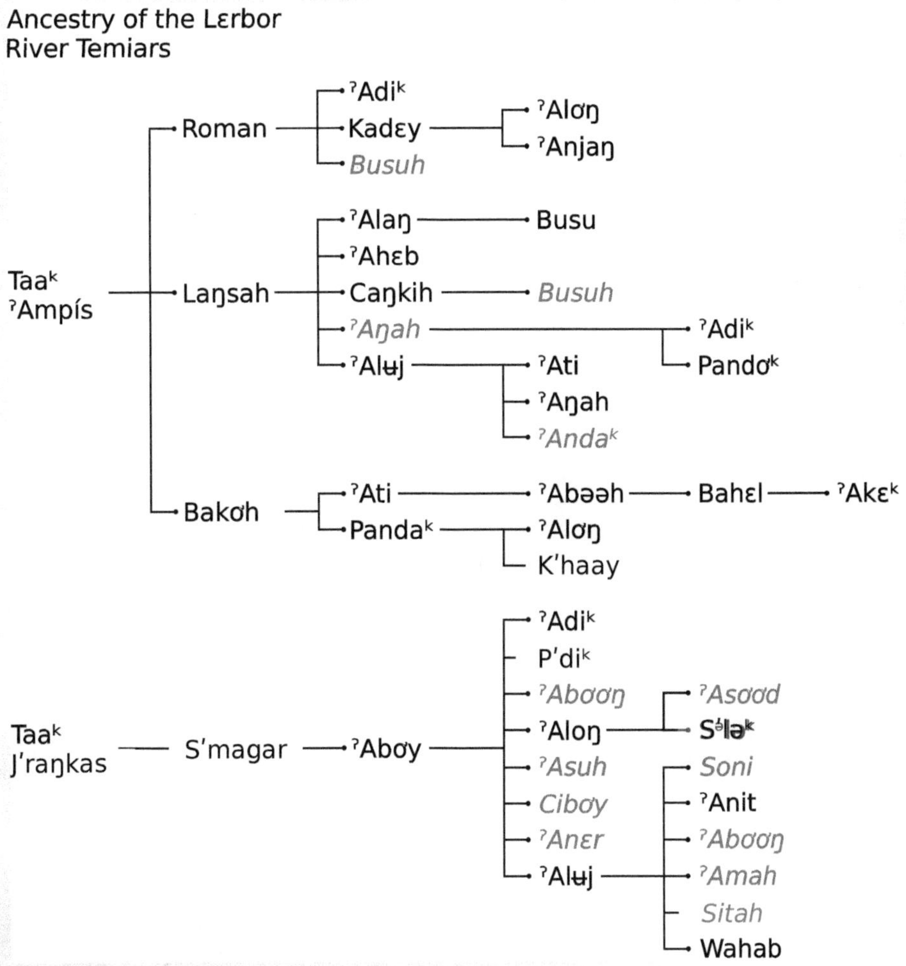

Ancestry of the Lɛrbor River Temiars

Fig. 13. Ancestry of the Lɛrbor River Temiars, living at today's Gawíín, Calɛɛr and Guwaaŋ villages. The ancestry is only partially complete for the descendants of Taaᵏ J'raŋkas.

8 | THE COMMUNIST INSURGENCY

8.1 FEAR, ANXIETY AND THE AERIAL BOMBING

The Temiars record that they have experienced four wars since the tranquil days of peace. The first, long ago, was the *P'raŋ Batax*, or War of the Bataks, when a fabled, sub-human people hunted down the Temiars to kill and eat them. Then came the *P'raŋ J'pun*, the Second World War, during which they saw hundreds of aeroplanes flying overhead and heard news of the Japanese taking command of the land downriver. After that was the *P'raŋ Samun*, or War of Bandits, which was the period when gangs of Chinese took shelter in the jungle to escape the Japanese, and carried out acts of violence on the Orang Asli. Finally it was the *P'raŋ Laŋoʹoy*, the Communist Insurgency, which brought with it certainly the longest and most permanent changes to the Temiars way of life.

Possibly the first real effect that the Insurgency had on the Temiars of the Puyan was the aerial bombing carried out by the RAF in 1954. Many swidden fields were targeted with heavy iron

An unexploded iron bomb, found at S'rijoʹoh, when it rolled onto the logging road.

ʔAnyɛh P'diᵏ points to a bomb crater at S'rijoʹoh.

Cannon shells found by Temiars after the attacks.

8.1 At the settlement of Kayaaᵏ, on the Píɲcớɔŋ River, an old woman was shot through the hand and blood streamed down her arm. This caused them to flee to the Bərtax River.

bombs to destroy what they suspected was a food production line organised to supply the Insurgents. Fortunately no one was out in the fields at the time, as they had all run for safety when the drone of approaching aeroplanes was heard. The weak bamboo long-houses were strafed with machine guns in the attack, leaving them shredded to pieces. Miraculously, only two people were known to have been wounded that day, due to broken bamboo.[1] At that, they took what possessions they had and fled up the valleys to the caves at **Lawaar, Sibɛyu**, and **Rɛnipuy**, to take shelter and they hid there for a few months. The Temiars at Lɛrbor fled up the B′laʔəər River to Capớg cave. Jaaᵏ ʔAndoᵏ, an old woman from the village of S′maliyɛx, died on the way to Capớg, in a small cave at K′maraᵏ, as she had no food. Everyone else was suffering from hunger at this time too and they ventured out from the caves to collect food, although most of their manioc had been destroyed, leaving them in quite a dire situation. Up to ten bomb craters have been counted in the area around Pos Gɔɔb, from Lɛŋraaŋ to S′rijớh, and some unexploded bombs have been found.

The inside of the cave at Rɛnipuy, where the Puyan Temiars took shelter, is spacious and dry. (Credit: Johan ʔAlʉj)

Rɛnipuy Waterfall, on the Ragas River, with the cave to the right of it where Temiars took shelter in 1954.

Guwɔɔᵏ Lawaar, a cave inhabited by bats, where the Bərtax River Temiars took shelter to escape the RAF bombing.

K'maraᵏ Cave, where Jaaᵏ ʔAndoᵏ died. (Credit, two pictures: ʔIdris ʔAsod)

Capo̓g Cave, where Temiars of the B'laʔəər River took shelter during the aerial bombing.

A serious incident occurred soon afterwards at the B′la²əər River. Three siblings who had fled to Capóg cave came down to their home at P′rəᵏ, when they felt it was safe to return, but they found everything in a state of destruction. While they were wondering where they should move to, a detachment of Malay soldiers, who had followed the track along the Puyan, descended on their settlement and started shooting. The three siblings fled and hid themselves in a cave at the river. The soldiers followed them and attacked the cave, killing all of them. Much later, an Orang Asli guide who had been with the soldiers reported to the victims' family what they had done, and this is how the story is known.

Before the bombing, perhaps some years earlier, an RAF Dakota transport plane had been circling the Puyan valley, which some say was broadcasting messages to the inhabitants below, urging them to leave the Communists and come out of the deep jungle. According to the Temiars, the old men who knew *halaaᵏ* cursed it because its noise terrified some of them. The plane flew toward the mountain and hit a tall *j′lax* (mahogany) tree with its wing, a short distance above the cascading Ləruw waterfall, causing it to crash into the river, killing all on board. At that time, the Píɲcóo'ŋ Temiars were staying at the Bərtax River, which was only a day's walk over Capaaᵏ and Bərlɛɛy mountain. But Taaᵏ Sisam was at Kayaaᵏ, with his son ²Abus (who today lives at Pinaŋ village) They heard the aircraft scream overhead and make a tremendous bang. When they went down to the river they saw there was blood in the water. A search plane flew over and spotted the crash site—a gaping hole in the canopy with all the leaves of the trees burned up. A week later a search party arrived on foot, led by Mat Yunus, a Temiar headman from Boóx B′tɰs (Kuala Betis), and guided by Temiars from Yaay and Símpor. Taaᵏ Sisam met Mat Yunus on his way and reported to him where the crash had happened. According to ²Abus Sisam, hardly anything remained of the crew, as the bodies had probably been removed by the tiger or other scavengers and the search party buried what little they found. Visitors to the crash site in recent years (by myself also, in 2010) could find evidence only the plane's tail section with twenty foot of fuselage and an engine and tyre, with the front and wings missing.

According to the lists of wartime crashes (found on-line), this crash happened on 25th August, 1950, and was of RAF Dakota KN630, of 52 Sqn, based at Singapore, which they say was possibly locating targets for bombers to attack at the time. Most of the reports state that the crash happened near 'Kampung Jenera', whereas in fact, it occurred near to Pinaŋ village, on the Píɲcóo'ŋ River. In 2008, two expeditions were made by the Malaysian Army, including a few British servicemen, to recover the remains of the deceased. Six local Temiars were employed as porters, but were each paid only RM50 (US$12) for their help. In the event of the dig, the Temiars were shocked to see how the dead were being disturbed but they said nothing. In 2014, the aircraft fuselage was washed away by flooding, and was completely flattened between logs left in the river by recent logging activities. Many small pieces of the aircraft have been found since in the river.

Left: Temiars of Píncoʻoŋ with the wreckage of the crashed RAF Dakota, pictured in 2010, before floods washed it away.

Below: The crash site after the floods of 2014. (Credit: Rapi)

During the whole period of the Insurgency, even up until 1988, when the last Chinese gave up, or had fled to Thailand, the Temiars lived in much fear. They kept their swiddens small and lived on fruits alone during the fruit season, to negate the need to work in the fields. They only lit the house fire at night, to avoid the smoke being seen in the daytime and inviting a bombing attack. Any news of danger, either from the Communists or the Army, would cause them to get up, abandon their homes, and flee to their hiding places in the forest. It is told that one family left their baby behind, hanging in a sarong cloth, out of sheer desperation to escape. The baby was soon found by a tiger which heard the sound of its crying. Another mother, in terrible fear of pursuers, caused her own child to suffocate, while she held its mouth to prevent it crying. They were hiding in a cave at the time and were fearful of the Army finding them, which they assumed was chasing them.

In 1955, the British Army commenced on a new strategy to expedite their war on the Communists —the gathering of the Orang Asli from their forest settlements, throughout the Central Range mountains, into safe zones that could be protected. This was a vital part of the war plan as the Communists were able to receive support from the Orang Asli in many ways, including an easy (or forced) food supply and also early warning of army patrols. In the Temiars' world, the communist fighters were not seen as an enemy as such because they had done them no harm in particular, although they had threatened them, on some occasions, with guns. The Temiars had little idea why the Chinese were there or what their aims were. When they encountered a settlement and asked for food, the Temiars provided it simply out of pity, just as they would give to anyone who was on a journey. They were not purposely supporting the Communists by feeding them, and they may also have been forced to cooperate. This corner of Western Kelantan served as a route onto Gerik, the Thai border and Barong. The Temiars were politically non-aligned, as their peaceful lifestyle warranted no need to fight anyone. But perhaps the Chinese had promised them a better life and had told them fables, saying that they had defeated the Japanese by themselves.

8.2   THE GATHERING AND RELOCATION

In **1955**, a group of Temiars, including **Panda*k T'roŋ**'s family, were gathered from their settlements on the Perak side to Ranah, an old swidden on the path from the Puyan over to the S'ŋaa*k River in upriver Perak. From there they were moved down-river all the way to **Batu*k Kato*k** and then to **Cɔɔs** (Malay name, Gua Cha). Later, the group ran off to **ʔUyas**, and then to **Pasíg**, then to **B'riix**, and over Sakoʼb mountain to **Pɛrloʼŋ**, eventually finding their way back up the Puyan and into Perak. They ran from Cɔɔs because the living conditions became unbearable. It was over-crowded and many were dying from an unknown illness. It is believed that certain Semais who were present there used harmful magic to kill them, and it is not the only time that the Semai have been accused of doing this—there was also a large death toll from a mysterious 'illness' during the stay at Jɛnɛɛs, a few years later.

In **1957**, the Home Guard arrived at the **Gɛrtu*k** River, Perak, and gathered the same group of Temiars again, back to **Ranah**, which had since become an SAS landing point (or LP). Another LP had been made at the Palɛɛs River, near its confluence with the Bərtax, in order to drop in troops to patrol the jungle.

Ranah

The mouth of the Lawaar River, at the Jɛŋhuŋ.

ʔUda Siyam stands in a former army dug-out.

The site of the camp at the gathering point at Ranah.

Army ration tins still remained on my visit in 2014.

Walking up Naŋkaaᵏ ridge, the path that Taaᵏ K'lusar used to reach Ranah from Lawaar.

The path to Lawaar from downriver, passing through K'rap Gully.

Evidence of the old swidden at Lawaar, a tree stump and wild secondary growth.

Messengers were sent up to **Taaᵏ K'lusar** at **Lawaar** and they instructed him to bring his group over the hill to Ranah. They arrived and stayed for ten days, in temporary shelters that they constructed just across the river. The Temiars helped to cut down trees to enlarge the landing zone. The helicopters were quite frightening and the down-wash of rotors also put out their fires.

They were soon joined by **ˀAlʊŋ Ramʊy's** group, who was living nearby at **Lɛrlǝǝr** and there was also a group led by **Taaᵏ Sagǝr**, brought over from **C'nɛŋduŋ**, at Ciyuŋ in Perak, but Sagǝr and his group were moved back into Perak afterwards.

Taaᵏ Snop (a British officer) told them not to fear their presence and assured them they were there to help them. **Taaᵏ Nun** (the name given to Richard Noone) was there and gave his embarrassed apology to Taaᵏ K'lusar for the earlier bombing of the swiddens (so I was told). He presented them with many gifts and foods, to assure them they were now in good care.

And of course, the Temiars, whose food sources had been either bombed or plundered, were quite happy to stay there and be fed, even though they hadn't seen such foods before. They were able to cook the rice, as well as oats and wheat grain, in bamboo tubes but the dried fish seemed bad as it was salty. They tried to chew on the anchovies without knowing they needed to cook them. They hit the sardine tins with the new bush knives to little avail, and they poured out the oil so they could use the large cans for fetching water. Sugar was boiled in water to make what must have become the sweetest nectar. Parachutes were cut up and shared out for blankets while the parachute lines were used to make fishing nets.

Other gifts included iron adzes, tobacco, salt, lipsticks, mirrors and beads. They tried eating the soap as well but were later shown how to use it for washing. They retained their clothing at the time, the men's *cawēēd* loin cloth with its tail, and the women's *ˀawēēd sʊʊg* wrap-around made of softened tree bark, and they continued to go bare-footed. They still ascertain today that this is the most stylish dress, especially for their dances, although they use cloth these days and not bark.

It was discussed among the British officers whether to move them over into Perak, but then the decision was made to bring them down into Kelantan. From Ranah they were taken down-river on foot to **Pɛrlʊŋ**—it was in April, because the millet crop had just been harvested. Then they progressed by bamboo rafts to the Puyan river-mouth, where supplies were air-dropped. The supplies were then carried by raft while the people went on foot up the Jɛnrʊl to the mouth of the **Rakíd** River. That year was the year of Independence of Malaysia. There was a *l'mog*, or former settlement at Rakíd, but it was overgrown and had to be cleared. They stayed there for two years, being fed to the full with army rations, including tinned cheese 'sausages', that they say tasted sweet. They also wore clothes here, for the first time in their history.

Taaᵏ Mudah B'jun's and **ˀAti Kabɛl's** groups were also gathered here from the Píɲcʊʊŋ River, and those from the B'laˀǝǝr and Lɛrbor Rivers were also gathered down to the Rakíd.

Alaŋ Pandaᵏ and **Bʊŋsu Pandaᵏ** were made the first Penghulus, or headmen, of the Puyan clan, along with ˀAlʊŋ ˀAlɥj from R'kʊʊb, when the people were gathered by the British Army in 1957. **Taaᵏ K'lusar** was made Penghulu of the Bǝrtax River clan, while **Taaᵏ Mudah** was made Penghulu of the Píɲcʊʊŋ River clan. It was Tuan Baye, a British officer, who flew in to set the

The rapids on the Jɛnrol, near Rakíd. (Credit: B'riix)

matter in order, and he first inquired of them from which river they each came and the extents of each one's *sakaaᵏ*. It was his intention that they should soon return to their homelands, under Army protection.

In **1958**, a logging license was granted the Temiars. It was first held under Pəŋhuluᵏ ʔAsim Suluŋ's name, but he went missing at Kota Bharu. So Pəŋhuluᵏ Cawan took the license. They cut timber at Rakíd, using their *jɛx*, the iron adze tied to a flexible handle, and they could fell one hardwood tree a day. The bark was stripped and the log was levered down the slope to the river, then tied with other logs with a raft of bamboo on each side and floated downstream. This went on for a year before they moved on. They also cut *taliᵏ riyo͝w* to trade, a small rattan.

Pəŋhuluᵏ Pandaᵏ felt that he couldn't stay at that place because the local Penghulu, named Cimbon, was jealous over his river territory and was quite weary of so many transient people living in his ancestral land. The Temiars recall that thern war a large group of people at the camp, with up to a thousand persons from the Puyan, and another thousand from the Jɛnro͝l River (they certainly could have numbered in the hundreds).

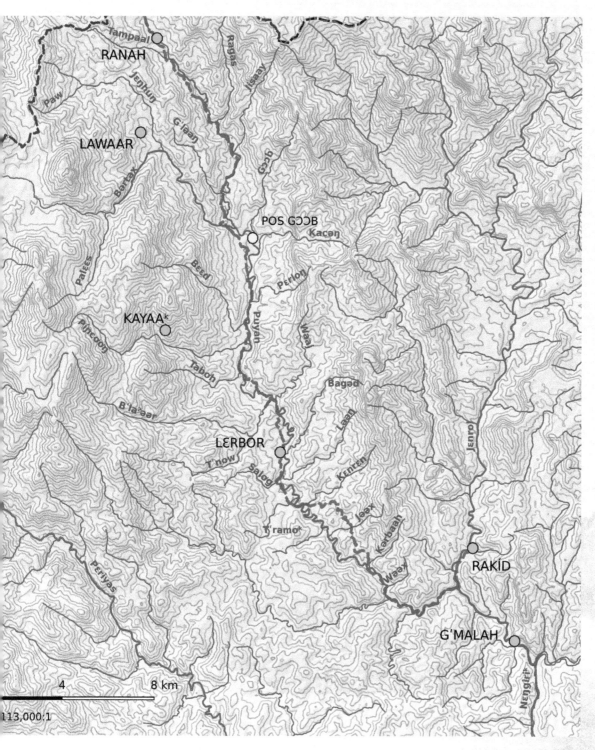

Fig. 14. Map showing the route that the Temiars walked from the Army landing zone at Ranah, down the Puyan and all the way to Rakíd, on the Jɛnrɔl River. The Different family groups were gathered from Ranah, Lawaar, Kayaaᵏ and Lɛrbor. A school was opened at Gᵊmalah in 1962.

In **1959**, they moved to the **Lɛrbor** River, where they stayed a year and also acquired rice seed at the time, which they were given to plant. ²Alaŋ Panda^k cut a swidden and planted rice for the first time since their return to the Puyan Valley, and no doubt others followed suit with their own swiddens.

In **1960**, the Puyan Temiars moved up-river to **Jɛnɛɛs**, which was named after a huge *jiyɛɛs* tree that stood there, near the **B'la²əər** river-mouth. They stayed there for four years, with the Senoi Praaq establishing an Army post there. The area was forested and it is said that two hundred or so Temiar men cut down the area with adzes to make room for the camp and the army base. A clinic was built and opened by Dr Bolton but many became sick there because the living conditions were too crowded.

Swiddens were cut to provide for each group at the settlement, these being at **Rɛnluŋ**, **Sisí^k**, **Jadɛɛr**, and **Pantɛy**. They built bamboo homes and each kin group lived around their own penghulu, or headman, of which there were five. The Army present included the *rɛjimɛn* (Malay Regiment), *gurkaa^k* (Gurkas), and *²askar sɛŋro'x* (Senoi Praaq), as well as the British Army.

In **1961**, young boys from the camp were sent down-river to be schooled at ²Uyas (Wias on maps) and in **1962**, they attended school at the old village of G'malah, which they reached by rafting down the Puyan, and they came home on foot. The late ²Uda Siyam was one of them. But there were social problems among the boys, as they mixed with others from downriver, and so none of them returned to G'malah after that and they had no schooling until the school opened at Gɔɔb, ten years later.

From Jɛnɛɛs the Temiars made foraging trips to parts of their ancestral land for hunting and fishing. K'lusar's group opened up the land at **Mɛnjo'o'n** to plant crops. Likewise at **Labu^k**, higher up the Bərtax River, because in that time the fish were plentiful and it was their homeland, where they felt free and spiritually whole. Fruit trees were planted at **Siyaduh**, and a durian tree still stands there today, but is visited by bears. Panda^k's clan, from the Puyan side, made camping, hunting and fishing excursions at **Cɛd²iid**, where he also planted durian and betel palms, and **Capɛɛr**, further upstream.

²Aso'd Boŋsu stands by an old bado'o'x tree (native rubber, jelutong), at Capɛɛr, which shows a gaping scar, testament to the tapping of its latex made over 50 years ago.

Rubber tappers' knives of the 1960s.

There were many deaths at Jɛnɛɛs due to sickness, especially among the children, and thus they were afraid of living there, in such a crowded place. Some moved away, not far, across the **Tabơh** River to the area of today's Kajaax village, but more died and were buried there too.

So the penghulus requested to move up the Puyan River, to an area within their former homeland and with more room to spread out. The Army then took the penghulus and other Temiars to survey the area at the Gɔɔb river. Thus, in **1964**, they broke camp at Jɛnɛɛs and shifted to the K'maar, Kacəŋ and Gɔɔb rivers, near the confluence of the Bərtax and Puyan rivers. The Temiars cut down the still forested area that would become the landing zone and Army fort. The British allowed them to move back up-river on condition that they would stay put there and not run off to Perak or any neighbouring valley.

Pəŋhuluᵏ K'lusar's people settled at **Lɛŋraaŋ**, **Tagɛɛs** and **Brawɛɛɲ**, on the west side of the Puyan, with Pəŋhuluᵏ ꞋAlaŋ's and Pəŋhuluᵏ Bơŋsu's clan living across the river from them at the Gɔɔb River, cutting swiddens at **Kacəŋ** and **Tapoɲ**. They planted many fruit trees, including durian and betel nut, and also rubber trees for the first time.

A rambutan tree that was planted at Lɛŋraaŋ, in the 1970s.

The graveyard at Leŋraaŋ, used for burials in the 1970s.

A giant rubber tree, planted by Pəŋhuluᵏ P'diᵏ, at Leŋraaŋ.

A tree stump at Tagɛɛs.

Timbul Pool, at the Puyan near Tapoʻŋ.

A jiyɛɛs tree at Tapoŋ.

The stump of a tree cut down by Taaᵏ Ramoy, at Tapoŋ.

The old swidden at B'rawɛɛɲ, reused in recent years.

Pəŋhuluᵏ Mudah's clan (from the Píɲcơơŋ River) moved with Pəŋhuluᵏ K'lusar and stayed nearby at **K'maar** Hill.

The Temiars originally from the Lɛrbor River (Lower Puyan) moved from the camp at Jɛnɛɛs back down-river, and settlied at the **Kɛnrɛn**. In **1968**, a new Pos was opened at Kɛnrɛn and **Sɛtiya Busu** was appointed the first Penghulu there.

At this time the British gave each Penghulu of the different rivers throughout the Temiar and Semai regions a single-barrel shotgun to take care of, together with many boxes of shotgun rounds. Each penghulu was also issued a gun license, which are still preserved today. These were made good use of for hunting monkeys and wild boar. Some of the guns still survive until today, having been cherished and repaired by their own craft-work (such the woven *c'noʊos* bands to hold the fore-piece to the barrel). But many have either broken or have been held by the police, who asked for them saying that they would help with repairs.

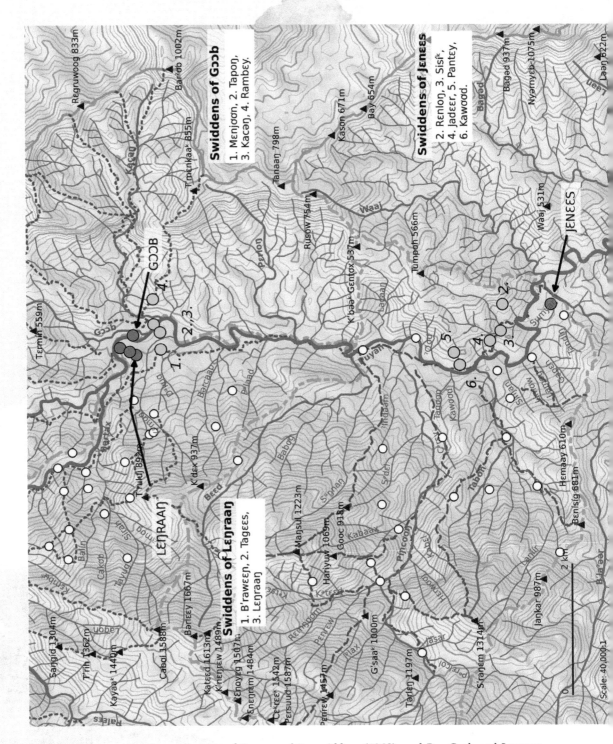

Fig. 15. Map showing the settlements of Jɛnɛɛs and its swiddens (1960), and Pos Gɔɔb and Lɛŋraaŋ (1964) with their first swiddens, further upriver near the confluence of the Bərtax with the Puyan River. Locations of the ancestral dwellings are indicated with white circles.

8.3 THE FORT AT GƆƆB

In **1964**, the Army established a fort situated at the Gɔɔb River, a small tributary of the Puyan, the plan being to give protection to the Temiars so that they would not support the Communists or be interfered with by them. The trees were cleared by the riverside to make a landing zone, while the fort was situated on top of a small hill over-looking the field below. Helicopters were then able to fly in with supplies, the round-nosed Westland Whirlwind being dubbed the *t'roŋ* (aubergine) and the long, twin-rotor Bristol Belvedere, the *balaᵏ* (hardwood log) by the Temiars present. Several Temiars were employed at the fort as mess servants, to wash the dishes and so forth, including Pandoᵏ Gɛndow (late father of ʔAŋah Pandoᵏ) and ʔAlʉj Sisam, who were only boys. Other villagers were employed to keep the area clear of wild undergrowth.

A helicopter run by the fire service, lands at Pos Gɔɔb in 2021, to deliver aid.

People wait at the Pos Gɔɔb landing zone to receive their food aid packages.
(Credit, three pictures: ʔAnɛl)

In **1969**, the Senoi Praaq were based at the fort and carried out training at Pos Gɔɔb. They made patrols from the fort into the surrounding mountains and also operated from forward bases such as Brabo, Labuᵏ and Palɛɛs. ʔAbus Sisam, of the Píɲcoʾoŋ clan, was enlisted in the SP and went through three month's training at Ulu Kintah, in Perak, before being posted to Pos Gɔɔb. A Malay CO, who was attached to another unit, was cross with ʔAbus, accusing him of not doing his duties. At this, ʔAbus said, "If you don't need me then, I'll go home." He left and returned to the Píɲcoʾoŋ, and later he heard that the CO who accused him had been replaced. It seemed that the Malay officers were not that favourable toward the Temiar soldiers and took opportunities to put them down. As it was, Malay, Indian and Singh soldiers were killed in action wherever they were sent, but of the *sɛŋroʾx*, no casualties were had among them. One Indian officer in the SP, Tuan Gunar, had thought that his amulets would offer adequate protection from bullets and it is told that he confronted a Chinese combatant, standing up before him, without fear. He missed his target and was shot dead himself.

Only one Temiar soldier was known to have been injured, when he walked into a booby trap, near Pos Kimaar. A convoy of five or six vehicles, heading toward Gerik one day, for operations in the jungle toward Terong, had been ambushed along the way by Communist fighters, who shot up all the cars. The SP soldiers jumped down to return fire. When they were counted up afterwards, none were missing. The Chinese called the *sɛŋroʾx* soldiers *askar cuwoᵏ*, or dog soldiers, because they never seemed to sleep, they were always moving, or they were always active at night. *Sɛŋroʾx* soldiers were completely acclimatized and accustomed to the forest and hunting in silence and stalking animals was second nature to them. Thus they proved highly adept at tracking down non-natives. Even the British SAS, who could survive three months without replacement, in the damp and darkness of the deep river valleys until their beards grew long, could scour the jungle up and down and not find anything. They actually began to wait for the SP to scout out areas first and then to go in when enemy camps were located.

In **1974**, the Senoi Praaq conducted recruitment at Gɔɔb. The special commando unit, that had been brought together under Richard Noone's planning, had proved very successful at rooting out the Communists from their jungle camps, and the Army wanted to increase their numbers. It is arguable that, if the Senoi Praaq commando unit hadn't been formed and deployed to the jungle, the Communists may not have been defeated at all as they had become more suited to the deep forest than any army unit trying to dislodge them.

8.4   CONTACT WITH THE COMMUNISTS

The following details were told me by the late Rtd Sgt ʔUda Siyam, at his home, in Kacəŋ village.

1954

Certain *Laŋoʾy* (actually the Temiar name for jungle ghosts) gave two shotguns to Bɔŋsu and ʔAlaŋ Pandaᵏ. When they met the British at the S'ŋaaᵏ River they threw them away but later they disclosed that they had the guns. From there they were taken to Ranah, along with K'lusar's clan from Lawaar, and those with Taaᵏ Ramoʾy from Kalaŋ, a settlement across the Puyan, to the east.

Then they discussed where to send them all, and the idea was to send them to Kimaar in Perak, but after a week they decided to keep them all in Kelantan. And so they all moved down the Puyan and that began the interim ten years of relocation, sickness and homelessness.

1973

Coming back from Pasíg, Pəŋhulu^k Boŋsu met Laŋoʻy who gave him 52 Ringgit and ordered him to buy them supplies. Boŋsu surrendered this money to an SB officer, but was then accused of lying as the SB didn't believe that Laŋoʻy were in the area, unless the villagers were harbouring them. And when armed searches were declared, it caused the Temiars to be frightened for their lives and they all fled for safety in the deeper forest. It took the Senoi Praaq to bring them back down again to their homes.

The late Pəŋhulu^k Boŋsu, in 2013.

Pəŋhulu^k Boŋsu's home at C'nantəl.

1973 - 25th November

Two Laŋoʻy, by the names of Akoi and Chow Chin, came to call recruits from the Temiars at Gɔɔb. They took thirty or more persons and reached as far as the Ciwɛs River in Perak, where they then sent back 21 persons because they lacked food. ʔUda Siyam was among the group from Gɔɔb and he also asked to go back (they didn't know he was in the Senoi Praaq because when they came to Gɔɔb recruiting ʔUda was on leave and not in uniform).

Fourteen persons went on to Thailand for training, in January, 1974. ʔUda had returned to Gɔɔb and he flew out by helicopter to Kroh, Perak (19th Jan, 1974), and from there took transport to Ipoh. On the Monday he reported to an SB Inspector, by the name of Mat Nor, and showed the where-abouts of the Laŋoʻy camp on the map. He was sent to Ulu Kintah to the Commando 69 unit.

The commandos readied and went by truck to Lasar, and by helicopter to Gɔɔb, in four units of men. The next day they moved up the forest track toward the border, camping on the way at the K'nɛgwɛg River. The next day they left six men at P'coʻh to make a landing zone. The group moved up through Ranah and up a mountain track to Jɛlmoʻl Tahoʻn.

Next day they reached Lancar, where they left six men. Thirteen men went on to the Jɛnraay, and found the Laŋoˈoy camp but it was deserted. At the Poˈdʔis River, there was a Laŋoˈoy hut, and there they left another six men. The seven remaining men went back to the Jɛnraay River. Then three members of Senoi Praaq from Poˈdʔis met Laŋoˈoy, who had come back from Betong, in Thailand, and they ran and told the seven at the Jɛnraay. So they followed, made contact and opened fire on them. One Malay soldier was hit and called on the Temiar soldiers to run, who were Kopi, Saitun, ʔAhíŋ and ʔAni.

During the withdrawal of the unit, a Laŋoˈoy hut was found at R′biŋ, which was full of dried elephant meat. The Malay soldiers ate the meat as they were hungry. ʔUda returned to the ambush site, at the R′biŋ River source. He carried on down to the R′biŋ confluence where they made a landing point. Three Laŋoˈoy returned to their hut to leave a message. One of them was shot by Pt Mandi, a Temiar. At the ambush site, ʔUda found a case of 300 point-303 rounds, plus a point-22 rifle and one Browning pistol.

1976

Pəŋhuluᵏ Boŋsu called Akoi and Chow Chin[2] to advise them to surrender their arms. As for the Temiars, it was getting hard, with both Laŋoˈoy and government interfering with their lives and the fighting all seemed so meaningless to them.

Only in 1989 did they surrender. But after all the hard work and effort and bravery that the Temiars had contributed, toward the demise of the Laŋoˈoy in the jungle, hardly any acknowledgment has been made of it. And, in the minds of the soldiers who put their lives in danger, their effort hardly brought any benefit to themselves because no official acknowledgment has ever been made regarding the rights of the original inhabitants of the land.

8.2 This Chow Chin is most likely the name by which Chin Peng, the leader of the Chinese communists, was known to the Temiars at Gɔɔb.

Latif ʔAbaaɲ points to jerry cans left by the army on the summit of P′naŋoˈw mountain.

9 | SETTLEMENTS IN THE POST-WAR ERA

This chapter details how the Temiar community of Pos Gɔɔb resettled their homeland in the years following the return from downriver, from 1970 until present. During this time the Temiars made quite a large shift in life-style, as compared to the early days when they lived in peace in the remote valleys, and were still wholly dependent on foraging and hunting, along with millet, without any processed goods reaching them. Army restrictions were imposed on them while they lived around the LP (Army landing point) and fort at Gɔɔb, and they couldn't roam freely or relocate to their former places in the upriver valleys or plant new swiddens too far away. There was an element of fear that hovered in the air and the slightest news of possible conflict coming their way would set off nerves, causing the Gɔɔb villagers to flee from their homes into deeper jungle.

The introduction of rubber and durian trees, distributed by the JHEOA (the then-named Dept for Aboriginal Affairs, which is now called JAKOA, the Dept for Orang Asli Development), perhaps helped to settle them into a more permanent situation. Even so, today's Tɛmagaaᵏ villagers have moved around between numerous village sites over the last fifty years, in the area of Lɛŋraaŋ, and likewise did the Píɲcơơŋ and Kɛnrɛn groups, downriver from Gɔɔb. For the Temiars living near the fort (of the Upper Puyan kin groups), perhaps it was more difficult to shift their homes from the vicinity of the fort because they would surely be missed, and they could only plant on the nearby hills, while staying put at Cadơơɲ and Kacəŋ.

9.1   KAMPUƋ TƐMAGAAᵏ

In 1974, the villagers took flight from Lɛŋraaŋ, due to the interference of the Communists, who had a camp at the Puɯn River, a mile up the Bərtax from Lɛŋraaŋ, and across the river from Labuᵏ. The Chinese had persuaded Pəŋhuluᵏ P'diᵏ and a crowd of others to join them and had made their camp the rendezvous. The Senoi Praaq were sent up to find them and they discovered them at the Puɯn, with no Chinese in sight. So they were brought back down to Gɔɔb, although some of the group had already left for Thailand. In the operation (in which the late ʔAndơᵏ ʔAti took part) the SP seized a sizable arms cache left behind by the Communists, amounting to 16 rifles and pistols, which was quite an unusual success.

The late ʔAndơᵏ ʔAti, a former member of the home guard, who discovered and confiscated communist weapons, in 1974.

The late Pandaᵏ ʔAlʉj, a former member of the home guard.

But in **1975**, with the Senoi Praaq having relocated to forward bases in the hills, leaving only Malay soldiers at Pos Gɔɔb, whom the Temiars called *pɛlpoʼs*, because they stole things, the villagers again took flight and disappeared up the mountain tracks. It didn't help that the Chinese SBO (Special Branch Officer), Tuan Goh Ahok, had accused them of harbouring the Communists, and announced that house-to-house searches would be conducted, and any Chinese that were found would be shot dead on sight. That felt much too close for comfort, with guns being pointed around in their homes, and so they fled. This was also the year that the British soldiers moved out, I am told, and this would have made the Temiars feel much less secure.

They crossed over the mountain path at Sɛmrajɛm, on the ascent of Pʼgʊy Mountain, and stayed at Rʼkʊʊb for two weeks. Then they made their way back over to Lawaar and it wasn't long before the Senoi Praaq found them and brought them down again to Gɔɔb.

In **February, 1976**, Taaᵏ Kʼlusar returned to Lawaar, with some of the village elders, as he felt he was near death and he wanted to end his life at the home of his fathers. With him were his sons ʔAlʊŋ and Pʼdiᵏ, Pandoᵏ Gɛndow, ʔAŋah Sɛdlij, Pʼdiᵏ Pandaᵏ (from ʔUyas) and ʔAlʊŋ Cɛrlʊy. The rest of the villagers moved from **Lɛŋraaŋ** to **Pɛltəl**, but some had already moved to nearby **Cəd** the year before.

The resting place of Taaᵏ Kʼlusar.

In **1977**, Taaᵏ Kʼlusar became ill and he died in September of that year. After laying his father to rest at Lawaar, Pʼdiᵏ returned to the **Lɛŋraaŋ** area and in **1978**, he was officially instituted the new penghulu of the Bərtax River Temiars.

In **1980**, they moved to **Sapɛd** where they dwelt for two years. This place, along with **Gʼləəŋ** and **Tampuy**, was a good hunting ground with good fishing and plenty of seasonal fruits (in the days before the loggers tore down their forest), such as durian, langsat, larah, rambutan and perah. At Sapɛd they planted cacao trees and even a coffee tree.

A tree stump stands at the old swidden of Saped, where rice was planted in the 1970s.

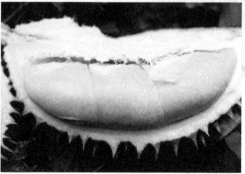

Durians have become a welcome source of food each summer, as the trees planted in the 1970s are now large and produce hundreds of fruits each.

Boys collect durians from the orchards at Píncʋʋŋ. (Credit: ʔAnɛl)

During the fruit season, some durian trees are harvested by knocking the fruits off the tree while still unripe. The white flesh is extracted and baked inside bamboo to make it soft and sweet.

When the fruit season is in full swing, durians are collected and sold to traders. (Credit, two pictures: ʔAnɛl)

L'cax, or rambutans, planted in the 1970s, are harvested by the sackful.

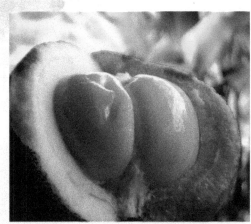

Rambɛy and rarơh fruits were also planted since the resettlement. (Credit: ʔAnɛl)

In **1982**, they moved back to **Pɛltəl** for a year, and then in **1983**, they moved to **S'tool**, where Pəŋhuluᵏ P'diᵏ and ʔAnjaŋ Sơid planted more rubber trees (the second planting).

In **1985**, they moved to **Tɛmagaa**ᵏ where they stayed a long while. In **2002**, they moved down to K'síj and **P'rigơy**, because they were told they should be closer to the Pos village so that JHEOA could build them permanent homes. But no homes were built at that time and until today the Tɛmagaaᵏ villagers have continued building their own from bamboo, sometimes struggling to collect materials, and especially since the loggers destroyed most sources of roofing palms.

In **2004**, there was what they called a *sunami*, or a massive flash flood from the Puyan, originating from the Ragas, a tributary of the Puyan. No homes were hit by the flood, but most of the river's fish were cast onto dry land and died. Because of that, the villagers moved to higher ground for a while, with those in the valley, at Gɔɔb, moving up to Tɛrmin Hill, and those at P'rigơy moving up to K'lɛraŋ Hill.

In **2005**, they abandoned P'rigơy, after they found blood scattered around the village and they believed an evil spirit had been aroused in the place. They moved to **Raaŋ**, but shortly after they settled there the same disturbance occurred and they abandoned the place again and moved up to **Kalox**, just above today's Tɛmagaaᵏ village.

In **2006**, they moved to Tɛmagaaᵏ again, and remained there up until 2013, when the village divided into four, with two villages above, **Tɛmagaa**ᵏ and **K'lɛraŋ** (across the K'maar River) and two more villages, **Bərcaap** and **Tɛrsaaŋ**, down by the Puyan.

In **2015**, the homes at K'lɛraŋ were abandoned and new homes built again at Tɛmagaaᵏ, when hopes were raised of having hydro electricity in the village (though the system, installed by an NGO, became defunct after a month of use). Tɛrsaaŋ was also abandoned (due to a *bɛrbơw* tree interfering with people's health) and the villagers built new homes at **K'rơx** hill.

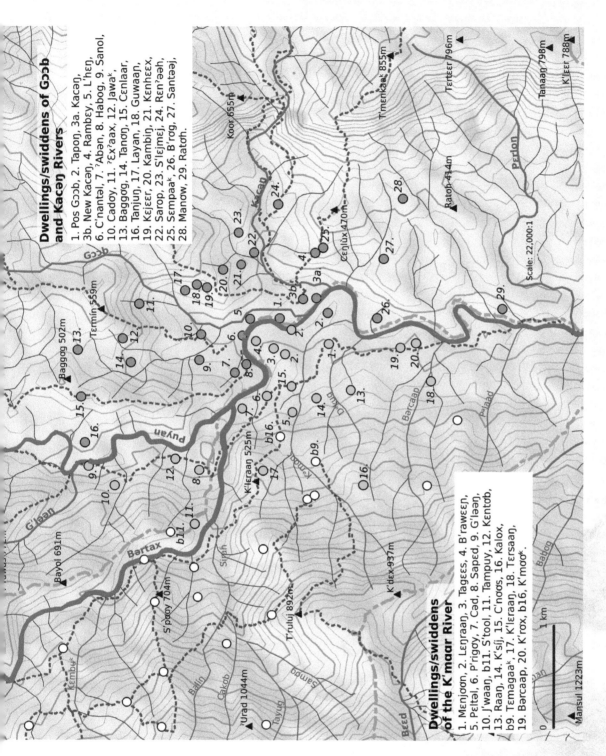

Dwellings/swiddens of Gɔɔb and Kacəŋ Rivers

1. Pos Gɔɔb, 2. Tapoŋ, 3a. Kacəŋ, 3b. New Kacəŋ, 4. Rambəy, 5. L'hɛŋ, 6. C'nantel, 7. ʔAban, 8. Habog, 9. Sanol, 10. Cadoy, 11. ʔƐxʔaax, 12. Jawaᵏ, 13. Baggog, 14. Tanoŋ, 15. Cɛnlaar, 16. Tanjuŋ, 17. Layan, 18. Guwaaŋ, 19. Kɛjɛɛr, 20. Kambiŋ, 21. Kenhɛɛx, 22. Sarop, 23. S'lejmej, 24. Renʔəəh, 25. Sempaaᵏ, 26. B'rog, 27. Santəej, 28. Manəw, 29. Ratoh.

Dwellings/swiddens of the K'maar River

1. Menjɔɔn, 2. Leŋraaŋ, 3. Tagɛɛs, 4. B'rawɛɛn, 5. Pɛltəl, 6. P'rigoy, 7. Cəd, 8. Saped, 9. G'laəŋ, 10. J'waaŋ, b11. S'tool, 11. Tampuy, 12. Kentɔb, 13. Raaŋ, 14. K'sij, 15. C'noos, 16. Kalox, b9. Temagaaᵏ, 17. K'lɛraaŋ, 18. Tersaaŋ, 19. Bɛrcaap, 20. K'rox, b16. K'mooᵏ.

Fig. 16. Map showing the settlements of the Bərtax and Puyan Temiars, from the time of their return to the Gɔɔb River in 1964, until present. Note that the Bərtax Temiars shifted from one place to the next whereas the Puyan group lived near the fort and cut their swiddens in the nearby valleys.

9.2   KAMPUŊ POS GƆƆB

Unlike Pəŋhuluᵏ P'diᵏ's clan, who have moved from place to place in the area across the Puyan from Pos Gɔɔb, at the K'maar River, Pəŋhuluᵏ ²Alaŋ's and Boŋsu's clan, together with Taaᵏ Ramoʹy's group, stayed located near the fort, at **Gɔɔb**, **Cadoʹoɲ**, **Kacəŋ** and **B'roʹg**.

Over the years, many swiddens were cut by them in the nearby area, for planting manioc, hill rice and millet, including those at **Ratoʹh**, **Manoʹw**, **Santəəj**, **Sɛmpaaᵏ**, **Rambɛy**, **Kɛnhɛɛx**, **Sarop**, **S'lɛjmɛj**, **Rɛn²əəh**, **K'jɛɛr**, **²Ɛx²aax**, **Layan**, **Guwaaɲ**, **Kambiɲ**, **Jawaᵏ**, **Tanoʹŋ**, **Cɛnlaar**, **Baggoʹg** and **Tanjuŋ**.

Today, the group of Puyan Temiars descended from ²Alaŋ and Boŋsu Pandaᵏ live close to the old Post, at **L'hɛɛŋ** and **C'nantəl**, a stone's throw from the Puyan River. Pəŋhuluᵏ Boŋsu, together with his son, ²Asoʹd, lived at **Sanol** for some years until they moved closer to the main river at ²Abən, and he remained there until his death, in 2014.

The group of Puyan Temiars descended from Taaᵏ Ramoʹy and Taaᵏ Ranah live today at **B'roʹg**, **Kacəŋ** and **Bərcaap**.

B'roʹg village

The burial of Boŋsu Pandaᵏ, in 2013, one of the first penghulus of the Puyan Temiars.

9.3 KAMPUŊ PINAŊ

In **1964**, Pəŋhuluᵏ Mudah and his people moved from Jɛnɛɛs to K'maar hill, which was ten minutes walk away from Pəŋhuluᵏ K'lusar's settlement at Lɛŋraaŋ. Some of the Píɲcơơŋ Temiars moved down to the Kɛnrɛn River, with Taaᵏ ʔAbaaɲ (who they called Taaᵏ Kawííb, because of his sun bear dream-guide) and remained there for five years.

In **1969**, they moved back to the Píɲcơơŋ River, together with those who had been at the Kɛnrɛn, and lived near the old Pinaŋ village location, down by the Puyan. The old betel trees that grew at the former long-house site, that give the place its name, had been cut down by passers-by, in order to steal the fruits. Here they planted rice on the hill side and also across the Píɲcơơŋ River. They attempted to make their home on the other side of the Píɲcơơŋ as well, at **Gərgɛg**, but the place was unsuitable and they moved back to the area above Pinaŋ. Some of them lived at the **Bɛɛd** River at this time, as well as **S'dal**, up the Bɛɛd River valley.

Cultivation of hill rice has become a way of life to the Temiars. Seed is planted in holes made with a dibble stick and later the field must be weeded to ensure that the rice produces full heads. The rice heads are plucked off with a small blade in the hand, while the stalks are flattened down with the foot.

Bananas, sweetcorn and pineapples are planted abundantly by today's Temiars.

The Army cleared a Landing Zone near Pinaŋ for operations. Sometimes the soldiers exchanged their rations with the villagers in return for manioc or fruits and some of them flirted with the young women. One soldier earnestly desired to marry a girl and even asked permission of the elders of the village, only to be denied by them, as they were afraid that their daughters would be taken away and never come home.

Pəŋhulu\k Mudah died while visiting relatives in Perak that year and **Pərdih Cɛnwah** was made the new penghulu.

In **1970**, the Department for Aboriginal Affairs, JHEOA, gave the villagers seedlings of durian, rubber, and sugar cane. The durian trees are still standing today at Pinaŋ, by the road, and dozens of rubber trees still stand and would be tapped if the rubber had any value this far from town. They also introduced goats and sheep (as well as at the other villages) but these proved an easy lunch for tigers and none of the livestock survived long. One river near Kacəŋ is named ʔOʹox Kambíŋ after a goat's carcass was found there.

In **1971**, a small clinic was opened for a short time at Pinaŋ, by Dr Bolton, to distribute medicines.

In **1973**, they lived at two locations on the Puyan, with ʔAti Kabɛl dwelling at **P'lad Hill**, and Pərdih Cɛnwah settled at **Pinaŋ**.

In **1974**, they took flight with the others from Pos Gɔɔb, when they became nervous of Army activities. They scattered about up the valleys and Pərdih's group fled to Ranah, high on the Puyan.

In **1976**, after Taa\k ʔAti died at P'lad, they moved to the **Sanol** River, and the next year a stone's throw away to **Pɛrlơŋ**, on the Puyan.

The late ˀAdiᵏ R'masa, with his wife, ˀAjɛɛw ˀAloŋ, at their home in S'maliyɛx. They were the last of their generation of Píɲcơơŋ Temiars. Both died in 2022.

S'maliyɛx, in 2014, a small dwelling surrounded by durian trees.

In **1978**, they returned to Pinaŋ, where the clinic had been. At this time they planted fruit trees down near the river-mouth, at **Lacaaŋ**. ʔAdiᵏ Rʹmasa moved back to **Sʹmaliyɛx**, on the Taboʰh River.

In **1985,** they moved down to **Tagoʼɲ**, along the land adjacent to the tiny Tagoŋ River, and planted many fruit trees there as well as across the main river at **Kawoʼod**.

In **1994**, they moved with Pəŋhuluᵏ ʔUsop up to the new Pinaŋ, on the hill-top above the former settlement where the clinic had been. The new village is called Píɲcoʼoŋ by most people, after the river, not knowing the history of the place. They moved here after the storm blew up because of the turtle that they had laughed at (refer to the story, Vol. 1, p7).

In **2002**, half of the village took flight because of a domestic issue, leaving Pəŋhuluᵏ ʔUsop alone at Pinaŋ. The others went to **Tɛmagaaᵏ**, and then to **Raaŋ**, where they stayed for two years.

In **2004**, they moved to **Kajaax**, to stay with Busu Loʼŋ. Busu, originally from the Píɲcoʼoŋ River, had come back from the gathering via Bʹriix, and Kʹləəd, settling at **Kayiix**, in **1997**, at the Taboʰh River. He moved to Kajaax in **2003**.

Pəŋhuluᵏ ʔUsop died in **2013**, from blow-dart poison that he drank, it is told, having been driven crazy by his Jehai wife (who may have cast a love spell on him, to marry him).

In **2015**, they moved back to the new **Pinaŋ** and built homes not far from where Pəŋhuluᵏ ʔUsop had lived, clearing some of the rubber trees to make more room.

The late Busu Loʼŋ, at his home in Kajaax.

The late Pəŋhuluᵏ ʔUsop, the last headman of Píɲcoʼoŋ village.

ʔAlơŋ ʔAlɨj, from R'kơʼb, had been living with Pəŋhuluᵏ ʔUsop up until **1992**, until he moved down to the **B'laʔəər** River, where he settled at the mouth of the T'now River. His son-in-law, ʔAyob Bərlɛy, a Bərtax Temiar, joined him there and the village of **Tanjuŋ** was made. They moved to **ʔAncơ̌h**, on the hill above, for some years before ʔAlơŋ returned to R'kơʼb and ʔAyob settled again at Tanjuŋ.

The homes of Tanjuŋ village, in 2013.

The graveyard at Tanjuŋ.

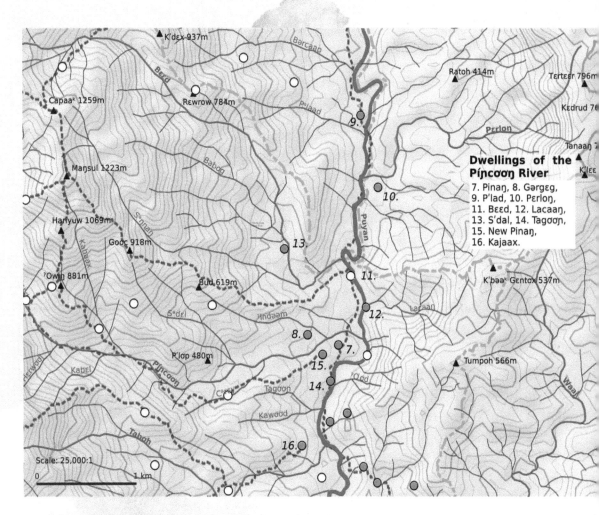

Dwellings of the Píŋcoʾoŋ River
7. Pinaŋ, 8. Gərgɛg,
9. P'lad, 10. Pɛrloŋ,
11. Bɛɛd, 12. Lacaaŋ,
13. S'dal, 14. Tagɔɔŋ,
15. New Pinaŋ,
16. Kajaax.

Fig. 17. Map showing the settlements of the Píŋcoʾoŋ Temiars, from the time of their return to Pinaŋ from Pos Gɔɔb, in 1969, until present.

9.4 KAMPUŊ GAWÍÍN

The Temiar clan fom the Lɛrbor River was gathered with the other Puyan River clans and relocated by the British Army down to Rakíd. From there they moved with the Puyan group up-river to Jɛnɛɛs and, in **1964**, they moved from Jɛnɛɛs down-river to the **Kɛnrɛn**.

In **1968**, a new Post was opened at Kɛnrɛn, together with a clinic, and **Sɛtiya Busu** was made the first penghulu there.

In **1970**, **K'haay Panda**ᵏ was made penghulu and he held the position until his death, in 2004. The Kɛnrɛn group of Temiars, headed by Paŋhuluᵏ K'haay, moved about from place to place, wherver it was suitable to reside. From Kɛnrɛn they moved to **Soroŋ**; then to **Kɛjwơj**; then to **B'luŋɛy, Kijɛl** and **Caad**; then to **Cɛlcol** and **Kərbaah**.

In **1996**, they moved to **K'ləəd** (at the K'ləəd River) and a new landing zone and post was opened. They cut swiddens at **Jaraw**, **R'lơy**, **Ləəŋ**, **Salơg**, **Pulɛy**, **P'laceᵏ**, **Rompay**, **Tihɔɔᵏ**, **ʔAhíŋ**, **Tajaar** and **Guwaaɲ**.

In **2002**, they moved (for nearly the last time) to **Kampuŋ Gawíín**. After living there all together for ten years, in **2012**, certain families moved from Gawíín and made two new villages down the hill, **Calɛɛr** and **Guwaaɲ**.

In **2014**, **ʔAkɛᵏ Bahɛl** was finally instituted as the new penghulu of Kampuŋ Gawíín, after ten years without a penghulu.

A great jiyɛɛs tree at the old village of K'ləəd. (Credit: Gawíín)

ʔAbaaɲ ʔAnjaŋ, one of the last survivors of his generation of Temiars, who also contributed much to the record of their history.

The late Bahɛl ʔAbəəh, cousin of the late Pəŋhuluᵏ K'haay, and father of the new Penghulu of Gawíín, ʔAkɛᵏ Bahɛl.

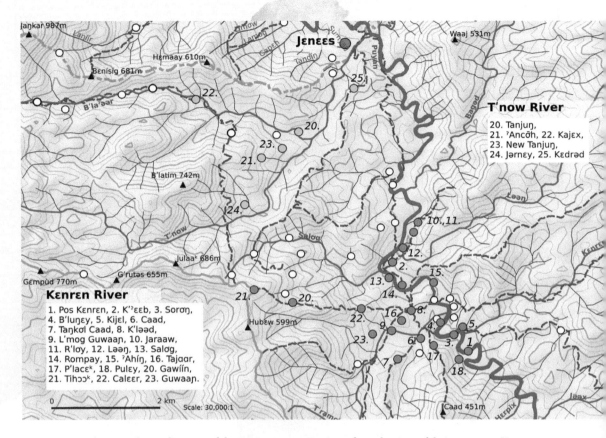

Fig. 18. Map showing the settlements of the Lower Puyan Temiars, from the time of their return to Kɛnrɛn from the settlement at Jɛnɛɛs, in 1964, until present, and also of certain Bərtax River Temiars who settled at the T'now River in 1992.

9.5 SCHOOLING AND EARLY HEALTHCARE

In **1968**, a school was built by the British Army (3 Troop, 11th Indep. Fd. Sqd.), along with a clinic and basic housing for teachers. The buildings were constructed from aluminum frame that was flown in and the skeletal remains of the clinic are still standing at the landing zone today.

The school was officially opened in **1970** and the first teachers were Temiars, ʔAnjaŋ from ʔUyas, and ʔAloŋ and ʔApah from Kuala Betis. They taught up to the year **1973**, because in early 1974, things were disrupted when the villagers fled up-river to Lawaar.

In **1975**, the British left and handed over administration of the fort with its community of Temiars to Malaysian authorities. Two double-rotor helicopters full of soldiers and officials flew in to Pos Gɔɔb to make their farewell.

In **1976**, Malay teachers took over the running of the school and they taught until the year **1986**. Typically, under their supervision, each day's classes lasted only from 9am until 11am. The school was closed at that point because the teachers or authorities said that it was too far to come to Pos Gɔɔb.

The memorial stone laid by the British Army, in 1968.

The aluminium frame of the clinic still stands at Gɔɔb.

The remains of the clinic at Jɛnɛɛs.

The structural frame of the clinic at K'lǝǝd still survives.

The clinic had at least one permanent staff person, who could deal with minor cases, but the doctor would fly in by helicopter to carry out health checks and the collection of blood samples for malaria testing. Serious cases could be evacuated by air to the JHEOA hospital at Gombak (the hospital near Kuala Lumpur, that was opened by Dr Bolton for the Orang Asli). The clinic closed in the year **1987**, but the emergency evacuation service by helicopter continued. A two-way wireless operator was stationed at every Post and many other remote villages, who listened in each morning for news alerts from other centres or could call in to arrange for emergency medical evacuation. The most frequent cases needing airlifting out were for child-birth, but there have been numerous accident victims needing immediate medical attention, such as of tree-falls, burns and other severe wounds.

Medical visits also continued by air, on a fairly infrequent basis, up until **2008**, when a doctor service began flying in to every village, about twice yearly. The doctor carried out pre-natal and medical checkups and dispensed basic medicines. This service lasted until **2017**, when it was replaced by over-land medical teams.

In **2004**, a doctor flew in and dispensed an unknown medicine to the entire community. This resulted in terrible skin conditions just the day after, with painful blistering all over their bodies. The blisters were described as balloons puffing up with fluid that needed popping to release the burning pain. Cockroaches helped a little by nibbling at them at night. At least two children died, suspected from ingesting the medicine through lactation from their mothers.

In the **1990s**, schooling for the children of Pos Gɔɔb was provided at the government boarding school at Pos Pasíg and this continued until around 2009. Children were collected from Gɔɔb but no transport was provided for their return, meaning that children often made the two-day walk home over the mountain pass each holidays or when running away. One teacher, known as Taiko, who was the boarding warden, was notorious for 'torturing' the children, screwing pencils in their temples, stumping them on the head with the end of a rattan stick (from which those children, now in their twenties, still carry the scars), and forcing them to stand up all night with the lights on. The eight to twelve-year-olds were hit on the head up to ten times each, until some of them bled from their nose and ears, but they were too afraid to flinch. They say that they couldn't think straight after that, let alone learn to read.[1]

9.1 Another time, while using the children to cut the brush back, this teacher ordered some of them to crawl inside a hollow ironwood log, perhaps knowoing that the Temiars are afraid of this kind of tree, and lit a fire at its mouth, which resulted in them getting ill.

This teacher would send them all to bathe at the river while it was in flood and one girl, by the name of ʔAtɵ́ɵ́s, went near a mud wall and it collapsed on her. The school staff arrived too late to save her, and she died. Another girl, ʔAlus, became very ill, due to the fact that the dormitories were built on a graveyard and the children were unknowingly playing on graves, and she died in hospital. Another time he ordered each class to lie down on their fronts so that he could stand on their backs, causing some children to gasp for air. The children became desperate to run away after that and they looked for ways to slip past the gate guard, who used to report on them when they sneaked out to find manioc roots to pull up when they were starving. When they did manage to escape, a loggers car took them up the mountain road, and they walked the rest of the way, alone through the jungle. On reaching home their parents scolded them for running off!

Later on, some children were able to attend school at Kuala Betis. But they soon gave up, and stopped going—the feeling of being held in a prison, away from their families, in foreign territory, and forced to survive on meager meal portions, while not learning anything at the same time, made them immeasurably homesick. They longed to go home during the fruit season so that they could satisfy their thirst for sweet fruits, which were ripening in their own orchards, but the holidays were at the wrong time of year for them. When they tried harvesting the plentiful rambutans near the school they were reprimanded for it, and were amazed how the locals wouldn't share with them.

Children from Gawíín were schooled at Pos Toho̓y, but they also ran away frequently. In 2015, five children ran out the back of the dormitory and ended up lost on the riverbank of the Pɛriyas, a fast-flowing river. One girl was wounded from a fall and she died while the others watched her. Another was swept away in her sleep by rising water and the remaining three survived on fern shoots for fifty days, before they were discovered.

Some children moved on to secondary school at Gua Musang town and it was only there, at the age of thirteen or fourteen, that they learned to read and write. The non-Muslim students faced constant pressure from the staff to convert to Islam, and were told that without conversion they would not be able to continue studies after their exams. The teachers would tell them each morning, that, as Orang Asli children, they should be happy with knowing the alphabet and shouldn't aspire to become anything, and that because they ate pig, they had little brains to learn with anyway. There have been no Temiar-speaking teachers in the last forty years (even when indigenous peoples have the right to learn in their own language, according to the UNDRIP). The children are forced to study in the national language, Bahasa Malayu, even when many of them struggle to speak it.

In **2014**, schooling was provided at J'rɛɛg, down the road from Pasíg, for those who had not continued schooling since 2009. Some children suffered from spirit-possession at the school, suspected to have been caused by malicious charms and due to their susceptibility while being far from the protection of their families.[2]

9.6   TIGERS AT THE PUYAN

Sometime in the 1970s, Pəŋhulu^k Bo̓ŋsu went up into the forest at Capɛɛr to look for **g'haru^k,** or 'agarwood', a wood with fragrant resin that can fetch a good price. Near evening time, he was on his way back and he heard strange sounds, as if people were talking. But he realised that this sound was evil (as tigers can make many strange sounds, such as of people chattering) and he quickly shimmied up a small tree and into a jungle durian tree, for safety. Shortly, he saw there were six tigers below, trying to climb up the tree after him. He had managed to take dry bamboo up the tree and he lit it with fire and threw it down on the tigers. He had to wait his time up in the tree and could only come down after being up there for a whole week. But because he knew *halaa^k*, he could forgo eating food for long periods if necessary.

The tigers made growling noises all that time and that is how the place, which was a fruit orchard before the loggers got there, obtained its name, Cɛd^ʔiid, which in Temiar means growling. When he came down he returned to his family at Sanol and told them not to go near there.

In **1974**, an incident happened while the group with Pəŋhulu^k Pərdih were harvesting *so̓ic* nuts at P'rawas Ridge, above the Bɛɛd River. It was during the fruit season and they were camping

9.2 The same problem has occurred recently, in May, 2023, at the Pos Toho̓y school, where at least four children have been sent home apparently spirit-possessed.

in different spots in the jungle to harvest and eat from the *jiyɛɛs* and *sɛmpaaᵏ* trees. At this camp they were collecting and grating *soʹic* nuts, and mashing them in bamboo tubes on the fire to make a hot-tasting cake. While they slept that night, lying along side each other, a tiger came in and took a man, by the name of ʔAŋah. When someone called the alert they all came out and chased the tiger away with spears. Taaᵏ ʔAŋah had broken *pɛlʔax* taboo, and so the tiger came for him.

In **1989**, Samsudin Bʹkəd had been up to Pos Gɔɔb one day, with his wife and four others, and was returning home to Tagoʹɲ. They rafted down-river from Bʹroʹg, on the rushing, brown water of the flooded Puyan. They drew up at Pʹlad to rest a while and suddenly they heard a bang that sounded like a gun shot. They didn't think much of it as they thought that someone was out hunting. But then there were more bangs along the river bank as they continued their rafting. They alighted at Bɛɛd and from there they walked down the river-side path to reach home, while strange noises followed behind them and a bird, the *cɛp tʹranɛᵏ*, which is known as the tiger bird, also made a few calls. They were afraid that one of them might have broken *pɛlʔax* blood taboo, and the tiger was seeking to attack them. They reached home safely, but in the night the tiger came and ate one of the dogs. This tiger was believed to be the late Taaᵏ ʔAti's *guníg*, roaming about looking for persons with the smell of offense.

While living at Raaŋ, in **2002**, Samsudin was out one morning to catch birds with gum strands, in the early hours before dawn. He first lit a fire near the tree, a *kɛriyɛɛh* fruit tree at Kʹroʹx hill, and then he prepared his *sɛɛp* strands for jabbing into the branches, the sticky black gum of which would cause the birds' feathers to stick together and make them fall to the ground. He climbed up the tree, while his seven-year-old son sat on a lower branch, and soon he saw two eyes below, glowing with the reflection of the fire. He hurried down, shouting, and grabbing a branch he hit the tree trunk to make noise, to scare off the tiger. It left, and he and his son waited in the tree until light. And this caused them to miss their bird-catching opportunity as, of course, none came to feed while they were still sitting in the tree.

10 | THE HISTORY OF LOGGING IN THE PUYAN VALLEY

10.1 "SINCE THE 1980S"

From the year 1968, when the Temiars returned to their original homeland and resettled the area of Pos Gɔɔb (and Pos Kɛnrɛn further downriver), up until 1988, a period of well-being and relative plenty was enjoyed in the Puyan Valley. That, of course, didn't come free of tension, as the Communists were still active and the Army based at Pos Gɔɔb was constantly restricting the movement of the Temiars, and any resemblance of peaceful life that they tried to pursue was often turned upside-down over-night. In the Temiars' mind, the temporary relocation downriver, lasting some ten or eleven years, even with its high death-toll in the camps, was a time put in parentheses. Their land still breathed life, even if they had been marched off it for a while, and coming back they found their heart was revitalised.

This twenty-year period was thus not too distinct from the time before the evacuation, and from the time that their forefathers roamed the land even. But the year 1988 marks the point in time when life took a change for worse and their years of tranquility were ended for good. That year saw the beginning of over 26 years of non-stop logging activities (from 1990 to 2016) that left their homeland a scarred mess void of hardwood in many areas.

Attachment to the land and its forest runs deep for the Temiars, as I have demonstrated in previous chapters. The forest allows them to maintain their identity as *sɛn²oͦy sɛŋroͦx*, forest people (even if they are moved out of it for a while), providing a wealth of raw materials, plants and animals from which they sustain life in natural and ritual ways. The abundance of forest resources all year round is the root of their happiness and contentment. But when these resources, habitats, and clean rivers are degraded and dirtied, then the Temiars begin to feel overwhelming loss. Ever since timber companies entered the Puyan Valley and began mashing the forest with their caterpillar tracks, the Temiars have experienced lack and scarcity in almost every aspect of their forest-dependent life.

Other Temiar communities have had it worse, however, such as those on the B'roͦx River, where they are surrounded by commercial plantations that reach to their doorsteps. For villagers of the various resettlement schemes (at Kuala Betis, Pos Tohoͦy and Pos Pasíg), a traditional way of life dependent on natural resources is now almost impossible to pursue. They are faced with the need to find basic employment, such as brush-cutting or loading oil palm fruits, in order to buy their rice and necessities. For them the fruits and fern shoots of the forest are long gone, the land available for planting crops is extremely limited, and freedom to cut and burn wherever they like no longer exists (they could be prosecuted for venturing into land which was once their own).

These plantations have not yet encroached into the Puyan, with their mono-crop of palms or latex trees and the herbicides that kill off everything else. But a large percentage of the land (I estimate over half the land area of the Puyan, of 28,000 hectares) has been harvested of its prime timber, causing a large and unrecoverable impact on the environment and the people whose homeland it is.

Majestic mahoganies once dominated the forest of the Puyan, but they have been cut down relentlessly in the last thirty years.

A Santaiwong lorry hauls logs past Tεmagaaᵏ village and a pile of logs at Soˀid Mountain.

It is hard to describe, in short, the impact that logging has had on the once lush primary forest of the Puyan, overflowing with biodiversity. The hardwood trees are the heart of the forest and the ecosystem they create under the cool shade of their canopies cannot be found anywhere else on the planet. Innumerable species of plants and animals depend on their towering presence, of the *j'lax* (*Shorea platycladus*, mahogany). the *r'guul* (*Koompassia excelsa*, tualang), the *cah* (Shorea sp.) and a hundred other varieties, including hardwoods (*bɛrbơw, laloᵏ, c'nal, bisɛh, mɛnraag, kolim, katùx, t'layax, tagɛɛs*) as well as fruiting trees (*mɛmhiim, tajaar, luwaaᵏ, g'tah cɛp, baay, bơt, lumag, maŋsul, p'rigơy, rakoᵏ, s'lɛjmɛj, tɛlbal* and many others) in order to thrive from the humidity and humus they provide. Take away this organ of the forest and nothing that was naturally around can continue to grow. Low-level plants die off in the exposure to direct sun-light and plants such as jagged angular fern and bamboo, once held in check by the dark of the great hardwoods, now proliferate and swarm all over the ground.

Trees standing nearby are shattered or stripped of bark and others left standing alone often keel over in the wind. The number of tracks the bulldozers make to extract logs turns the area into a spider-web of bare earth and uprooted palms. The forest floor, once a place of diverse natural species, that no man could have planted, providing for hundreds of traditional uses, is churned up by machinery. The hill-tops are not spared either, as the iron caterpillars crawl up them for every last desired tree trunk. Up the ridges they drive, following the ancient human paths which once were the arteries of travel in the forest. In a few years these tracks become so massed with bamboo and ferns that they are impossible to use. Other tracks cut across the old paths creating terraces, with high banks that must be climbed up using a pole.

Some plants can make a come back, and particularly if enough unwanted (defective) trees were left standing which then attempt to make a low-level secondary forest, and the Temiars can still forage for edible ferns in some areas, although now it depends on chance and luck to find anything. Primary forest, with all its resources, its medicinal plants, rattan vines, and ritual plants, is two or three hours' walk from home, instead of just outside the village. Hunting nearby is never successful as the animal habitats have been lost and only the wild boar remains that must be trapped. In the old days, Temiar men could take their blowpipe on any walk and shoot squirrels, civets and langurs, but now a hunt takes a day's venture or a few days of camping, and the animals might not be found anyway.

Logs clutter the Jɛŋhuŋ River, near Lawaar.

It is ironic that wildlife conservation agencies visit and stress the need to protect wild animals, when it has been the rampant deforestation that has caused the reduction of animal numbers. Villagers are told they cannot use a casting net at the river, because the fish population has so decreased, and yet this decrease has nothing to do with the native inhabitants and their fishing activities. In times past, sackfuls of fish were caught and bamboo weirs were constructed on which to strand fish, and yet with these methods the river pools were never depleted. But ever since logging roads made the way for outsiders to reach upriver regions, these rivers have been under a constant rate of interference. Firstly, the loggers, and other travelers, bombed or electrocuted the fish, scooping out the stocks of Malayan mahseer from the deep river pools. Then, as logging activities reached the hills surrounding the river valleys, landslides and heavy soil erosion were common place and millions of tons of sand soon deposited in all the rivers, creating shallow water and flushing out the fresh water ecosystem with the tsunami-style flash-floods caused by the lack of rain absorption on those bare hillsides.

Thus, with all these damages made to the environment, one can easily understand why the Temiars feel that life since the 1980s has been worse for them. The icons of their forest have been cut down and dragged away. The rivers are littered with logs and shallow from sanding. Wild animals are harder to find, except for pests, which lurk in dense undergrowth and destroy crops at night. Food is generally harder to come by, with fish now scarce and the fruit trees that used to support primates and birds having disappeared. Building materials are harder to find and sources of roofing palms have been permanently destroyed in places where they once flourished.

The Temiars' once ample supply of roofing palms, on the hills of the Pɛrloŋ River area, was destroyed by bulldozers during logging operations, as the logs were extracted and dragged over all the nearby vegetation.

10.1 Villagers harvested rattan recently, in 2023, to sell it at the 20 year old price of RM4 per 9ft length; one person made only RM700 for 200 pieces.

Life itself has become difficult to sustain and chores deemed less necessary are put off due to hunger and lack of energy. Today there is a shift of dependence toward bagged rice and processed products such as sugar and oil, whereas before, it was possible to find sustenance from the abundance all around. And with few means of making income the Temiars have become semi-dependent on government hand-outs and other charity, seeming to live off one subsidy to the next. In recent years (2010-2019), the trade of medicinal herbs, rattan, rubber, and durian fruits fetched only pitiful or rip-off prices.[1]

10.2 THE LOGGING OF THE PUYAN

In 1980, a Chinese trader by the name of Tokeh Ahing began seeking forest wares in the Puyan region, including *riyoʼw*, *manoʼw* and *haag* rattans, as well as *badoʼox* (jelutong, native latex), for which he held licenses to trade. The wares were rafted down-river to the trading point at Bertam. He also held a license to trade in *bala^k*, or hardwood, and his timber activities began at ʔUyas and Pasíg, during the 1980s. After his death, his son disposed of these licenses to other traders, the rattan trade to a Malay, named, Ma'eh, and the *bala^k* trade to other Chinese. By 1988, a road had been built from Pasíg that crossed the Puyan River at its lowest point, paving the way for the acquisition of hardwood from this river region. A kongsi (Malay for loggers' yard) was made there by the Chong Yu company.

A shrewd tactic was used by the loggers and they sought out all the headmen, including those from Pos Gɔɔb, P'di^k K'lusar, Bɔŋsu Hɛlwəd and K'haay Panda^k of Pos Kɛnrɛn, as well as the headmen from the Pos Símpor region, to obtain their thumb-stamps on a paper agreement. The story was that the company was preparing to build roads to the villages and nothing was disclosed about their plans to cut timber in the region. Following this, the villagers dispersed all over to cut rattan in anticipation of a road and arrival of traders.

It was ʔAwɛn P'di^k, else known as Taa^k ʔAwíís, the then headman of Pos Bihay, who led the way for the logging company at the time, easily convincing the village heads that this plan was in their best interests while failing to disclose the real purpose of the thumb-stamping. In one swift move, he sold off all their land for an unknown lump of cash and it is reported that he continued to work in this way whenever the opportunity arose, until, due to complaints, he was forced to move to Gerik in Perak. Many locals suspect that he used the Kijang Mas cooperative, that he was manager of, as cover for his land-trading activities. The cooperative was set up to help village communities sell their crafts and is based in Gua Musang.

Signs of past logging activities such as these are found all over the Lower Puyan.
(Credit: Wahab ʔAlʉj)

It is interesting that some logging companies have sought consent, in some form or other, from the Temiars, before commencing their operations, while some have not and have prefered to intimidate. Officials from the Kelantan Timber Association (KPK) have held numerous discussions with villagers (once with the police participating, at Kajaax, July 2016), explaining that the logging company has full rights to the timber, due to the license in their possesion. The loggers' arguments are always the same: they say they have paid so much money to the government and it will be wasted if they are delayed, they need to support their children going to school and how can they live if they are out of work? The Temiars explain every time that the forest is the home of their ancestors and that they need it to survive, and any logging activity will pollute their water supply for years, but their arguments never seem to matter.

In 1989, a company named 'Haji Mak' operated from the Puyan river-mouth, reaching the mouth of the B'síír River, while at the same time logging operations were being carried out in the locality of the old village of Gəmalah, where the first school for the Temiars had opened in the 1960s.

By 1992, the same company extracted timber at the Hooŋ River (between the Wəəx and Kərbaah Rivers), while also, logging operations had commenced at the R'kơơb River, Pos Símpor.

A logging boss tries to assure villagers at Kajaax, that not too much forest will be cleared in their river-source area.

Logging bosses bring along the police to help explain that their logging license gives them undeniable rights to cut down timber in the Temiars' customary land. (Credit: Rapi)

In 1995, a road was built from B'riix, at Pos Pasíg, that crossed into the Puyan valley at the T'hòʊr pass, between the rocky outcrops of the ʔAyaap and T'hòʊr hills, reaching the Bagəd River.

In 2001, the road was extended along the ridge over Tanaaŋ and T'mɛnkaaᵏ hills and into the Kacəŋ river-head area, directly east of Pos Gɔɔb. Thus, the first logging activities began in the Upper Puyan and they worked at the Bɛɛy, Gasɛᵏ, C'rɛɛm and Barʔòʊb Rivers, felling prime forest within the traditional hunting and foraging land of Pəŋhuluᵏ Bɔŋsu's people, without their full understanding or consent.

A felled tree near Barʔòʊb mountain.

A signboard placed at a log dump, at Tanaŋ, in 2003.

Landslides scar the land where loggers took all the hardwood, at T'mɛnkaaᵏ.

The former village of Pɛrloŋ was turned into a loggers' yard.

Intelligent tree planting: meranti trees planted by the Forestry, at Tanaaŋ, all in one spot! No trees have been planted in the more devastated areas.

In 2000, a company named 'Pangkam,' which had carried out logging operations at B'riix and the Pɛriyas River, commenced logging from the Hooŋ River (Lower Puyan), reaching the Jəəx River by 2004.

In 2001, a company named 'Abon' continued operations from the Bagəd River, and reached the Waaj River in 2003.

In 2002, a kongsi was built at the old village of Pɛrloŋ and, in the next three years, the areas of the Pɛrloŋ, Kɛdrud, Ratơh and Santəəj Rivers were logged out.

Logging activities reached the K'ləəd River via the road from Jadɛɛr (Pos Símpor) initially, and this extended through to Bɛɛd, from where a road was made that reached all the way to Tɛmagaaᵏ village (a higher road than today's Puyan valley road).

In 2005, Lamơg River was reached by the loggers and a kongsi was built at the former settlement of Jɛnɛɛs. From there the old villages of S'maliyɛx and Bagan (on the Tabơh River) were logged out. In 2006, a road was bulldozed up to Ləruw waterfall.

In the same year, the company named 'Kesuma Kota Bharu' logged out the lower Kacəŋ River areas of Rɛnˀəəh and Baggơg, operating from a kongsi built at Gasɛᵏ, on the Kacəŋ.

In 2006, the company named 'Bumi Timber Enterprise' built a kongsi at the J'rɛnˀiin River on the Waaj, and in the next three years it logged out the area of the old village of Lɛrbor.

In 2007, the company 'Wealth Will' operated from a kongsi at P'rəᵏ, and the areas of K'maraᵏ, up to Batuᵏ Jaŋkar ridge (at the B'la²əər River), and Mɛmhim (at the T'now River) were logged out.

By 2008, Labuᵏ and Bɛɛd were logged, from a kongsi built at the Píɲcơơŋ River.

In the same year, the company 'IEZ Ent' logged out the areas of P'lad, Rɛwrơơw, Lɛŋraaŋ, Tɛmagaaᵏ and Kalox.

In 2009, the companies 'AS Timber' and 'Emas Jaya' logged out the areas of K'lɛraŋ, T'ramơᵏ and T'ruluj, on the hills above Tɛmagaaᵏ, for two years.

In 2010, the company 'Nural Amin' logged out the areas of Sapɛd and G'ləəŋ, turning a once beautiful hunting ground into a mess of tracks and sprawling undergrowth, with much land erosion.

In the same year, operating from a kongsi built at Calyɛx, an old swidden on the Bərtax River, the company 'Abha Jaya' logged out the areas of L'bíír and Sajaaᵏ, at the Jɛŋhuŋ River, on the east side of Sơid mountain. The access road being cleared along the ridge line between the Bərtax and Puyan valleys, taking all the timber along its sides with it.

Deep soil erosion scars the hillside at Sajaaᵏ, after a company reached deep into the Jɛŋhuŋ River area, in 2013.

In 2011, the company 'AS Timber' carried out operations from the K'ləəd River until the Kajɛᵏ, with their kongsi built below the hill of Gawíín village. Also, the K'rɛitəy and Səmnaŋ Rivers, in the area of the Píɲcơơŋ River, were logged out from a kongsi at Bɛɛd.

In August of that year, the peaceful beauty spot at Ləruw waterfall was completely trashed when a large group drove up there and cut down all the giant bamboo growing in the area, in order to construct a temporary campsite. Apparently, their intentions were to start up tourism to the waterfall and P'naŋơw mountain, while by-passing the permission of the local Temiars. The matter was reported to the police by locals, at the consent of Pəŋhuluᵏ P'diᵏ, and the project was abandoned.

In 2013, the Bɛɛd and Sirah river-sources were logged, causing massive land slides above the Bɛɛd, and at the same time a road was bulldozed through Lagoh, S'lipɔɔh, and over the Bərtax River into Sơid mountain, where prime forest still stood.

In the same year, the company 'Air Bakoot Ent' logged out the remaining wood at K'ləəd.

Logs sitting at the Bɛɛd River, that were at first seized by the Forestry, as 'haram' wood, harvested outside the licensed area, but were later collected anyway.

A landslide at the Bɛɛd River.

J'nulaŋ Hill, in the foothills of ʔAbơơŋ mountain, deforested.

In the same year, the company 'GMS Timber Trading,' operating from the kongsi built on the site of the old Army fort at Pos Gɔɔb, reduced ²Abơơŋ mountain and its foothills to bare earth, with scattered lone-standing trees and tons of debris of wood and rocks pushed into the small rivers.

In 2014, the company 'Raswood Trading,' based at the kongsi built opposite B'rơg village, carried out rampant logging on Sơid mountain, on its South side, facing the Bərtax River, destroying pristine and unexplored virgin forest and turning its once beautiful ecosystem into complete chaos.

A girl from Tɛmagaaᵏ village, Saŋgíl Rahim, granddaughter of Pəŋhuluᵏ P'diᵏ, was lured into prostitution at the loggers yard at B'rơg. The foreign loggers gave her something to smoke and it ruined her mind, and some say she become spirit-possessed. She lived in the dirt under the house for the rest of her life and waned away, until, sadly, she died.

The loggers' yard that was situated right opposite B'rơg village. The close proximity of machinery and logs posed many dangers to the villagers. (Credit: Yusman ²Andoᵏ)

Machinery at Sơid mountain.

A bare earth strategy at Soɨd mountain. All natural plant species destroyed by wide open bulldozing.

At Soɨd the loggers cleared out all the great trees in the once untouched and unexplored primary forest that was full of diverse natural plant species, many which had medicinal value to the Temiars or provided food for wildlife and humans. Huge open areas were cleared and left as bare earth for wild undergrowth to take over. This kind of operation has continued unchecked by the forestry department, even though there are supposed to be guidelines that companies must follow and also the fact that deforestation has undoubtedly contributed to the massive flooding in the lowlands each rainy season.

Also in 2014, J'lantíís, Hɛnwơớc and the ridge from the G'ləəŋ River were logged out, bringing total destruction to yet more lush, prime forest, full of valuable resources, such as *manaa*r (the rafflesia vine flower bud).

Again, in 2014, operating from the kongsi built at the Ləruw waterfall, the company named 'Perkayuan Chengal Emas' logged out the upper Píɲcơóŋ River area, causing devastating effects as huge landslides of the rocky soil occurred after the ensuing heavy rains.

In 2015, the same company took a year to completely log out Sisíᵏ and Cabol, two hills across the Puyan from Pinaŋ, to the dismay of the local villagers.

Logs at Cɛdʔiid, once a fruit orchard that Bơŋsu Pandaᵏ planted in the 1970s.

J'lantíís, reduced to a wasteland.

A log pile on G'ləəŋ Ridge, once a hunting ground of the Temiars.

A huge landslide at the Rɛmŋoʻoʻm River, in the Pĩ́ncoʻoŋ water catchment.

Catastrophe at the Pɛnrɛɛw River. A whole valley is wiped away after heavy rain and flooding, due to the lack of trees to hold the rocky soil.

The crossing on the Puyan River, made by the loggers to reach Cabol.

The bare hilltop of once forested Cabol Hill.

Another land collapse caused by logging in the Píncoʻoŋ River source area, that has only lead to heavy sanding of the rivers downstream.

Giant logs are loaded at a log dump, near Gawíín, and hauled away.

During 2014, the company 'Prestij Mega Venture' carried out operations in the Waaj and Lacaaŋ River source areas, cutting down all the remaining small trees as if to prepare the land for a commercial plantation. The area of Kɛdrud and Pɛrloŋ was entered again in 2015, where roofing palms vital to the Pos Gɔɔb Temiars were mashed to pieces under iron caterpillar tracks. Their activities ceased in 2016 due to the Temiars' blockade on the main access road to the Puyan.

Also in 2015, the company 'Souncern Timber,' operating from the kongsi at Rɤndoŋ, logged out the hills of S'nawəər and the area of the Cɔx River, near the Puyan, for two years, causing further grievance to the people of Pos Gɔɔb.

Logging aftermath and a log pile at the Pɛrloŋ River.

Logs of small trees in the Waaj river-source area.

A log pile in the Cɔx River area.

In 2016, the mountainside of Rɛgruwɔɔg was cleaned out, with discreet access coming from the Bayuur River, over the ridge in the Pos Pasíg region.

In the same year, more work continued at Lǝruw, by a company called 'Swasta Sprint', after the blockade was broken down by the authorities that February.

In January of 2017, work continued at Lǝruw after the heavy rains were over, with the loggers preparing to cross the Píɲcoʻoŋ and cut down the remaining prime forest at Kayaaᵏ. Their work was hampered after a driver was killed when his car overturned and it was halted after a new blockade went up on the road near Tohoʻy.

Further logging above Lǝruw waterfall caused serious problems for the water supply of Pinaŋ village below. (Credit: Rapi)

In 2018, the loggers returned and repaired their kongsi at Lǝruw and aimed to extract the logs they had cut down the year before but continual rains hampered their work.

In 2019, the loggers showed up again to start more work at Lǝruw. They built a camp at the Taboʻh River and had the appearance and attitude of hired thugs. One villager from Píɲcoʻoŋ was injured when they blocked his way across the bridge and then pushed his motorbike into a car. Their work was soon disrupted when Perlilitan, the wildlife protection agency, came in and arrested most of them for trapping protected bird species.

Up until the present, trees have been marked by the Forestry Department for removal in the forests of Capɛɛr, Bagan, Siruy, Ragas (upstream Puyan), Sirah and Kɛmbʉᵏ (along the Bǝrtax) and Kayaaᵏ (upstream Píɲcoʻoŋ River). They will probably not stop until they reach the Perak border, unless local protest action can succeed in preventing them further, or the government intervenes and halts the issuance of logging licenses. Unfortunately, however, the forest is seen as a viable economic resource, and even when it is marked as Hutan Simpanan Kekal, or permanent forest reserve, it is only held back from commercial uses until the time when it is deemed ready for development.

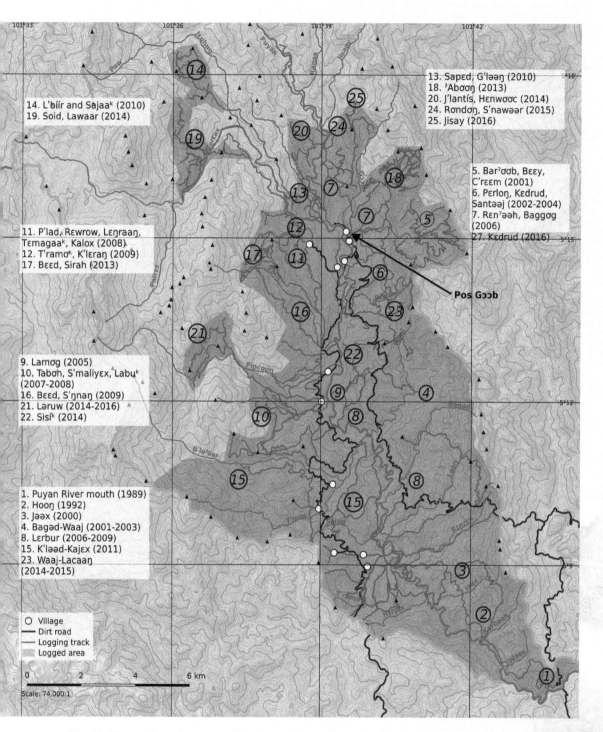

14. L'bíír and Sajaaᵏ (2010)
19. Soid, Lawaar (2014)

13. Sapɛd, G'ləəŋ (2010)
18. ʔAbσσŋ (2013)
20. J'lantís, Hɛnwσσc (2014)
24. Rσndσŋ, S'nawəər (2015)
25. Jisay (2016)

5. Barʔσσb, Bɛɛy,
C'rɛɛm (2001)
6. Pɛrlσŋ, Kɛdrud,
Santəəj (2002-2004)
7. Renʔəəh, Baggσg
(2006)
27. Kɛdrud (2016)

11. P'lad, Rɛwrow, Lɛŋraaŋ,
Tɛmagaaᵏ, Kalσx (2008)
12. T'ramσᵏ, K'Iɛraŋ (2009)
17. Bɛɛd, Sirah (2013)

Pos Gσσb

9. Lamσg (2005)
10. Tabσh, S'maliyɛx, Labuᵏ
(2007-2008)
16. Bɛɛd, S'ŋŋaŋ (2009)
21. Ləruw (2014-2016)
22. Sisíᵏ (2014)

1. Puyan River mouth (1989)
2. Hooŋ (1992)
3. Jəəx (2000)
4. Bagəd-Waaj (2001-2003)
8. Lɛrbur (2006-2009)
15. K'Iəəd-Kajɛx (2011)
23. Waaj-Lacaaŋ
(2014-2015)

○ Village
— Dirt road
— Logging track
▓ Logged area

0   2   4   6 km

Scale: 74,000:1

Fig. 19. Map to show the extent of logging activities (forest that has been harvested) in the Pos Gɔɔb
territory. The land amounts to an estimated 14,400 hectares out of a total of 28,000 hectares.

10.3   DAMAGES CAUSED BY LOGGING ACTIVITIES

1. **Grave sites destroyed by machinery, even though some of them showed clear signs of burials, having burial items laid on top:**
   - Bərtax: Kʼlɛraŋ, Lʼbíír
   - Pos Gɔɔb: Bʼrơg, ʔAbən, Cadơơɲ, Rondơŋ, Jʼlantíís, Cɛnrơᵏ, Cɔx, Ratơh
   - Píɲcơơŋ: Jɛnɛɛs, Pinaŋ
   - Lower Puyan: ʔɛndiŋ, Lɛrbor, Pʼrəəᵏ, Kajɛɛᵏ

2. **Plantations bulldozed to make roads or destroyed while removing hardwood:**
   - Rubber trees at Lɛrbor, Kʼləəd, Taɲjuŋ, Tɛmagaaᵏ and Calyɛx
   - Fruit orchards at Taɲjuŋ, Pɛrlơŋ, Santəəj, Bʼrơg, Gɔɔb, Cadơơɲ, Gʼləəŋ
   - Cacao trees at Kajaax
   - Banana trees at Bərcaap, Manioc at Lagoh

3. **Hundreds of fruit trees that were important food sources for animals and humans, were cut down for timber, including:**
   - Durian (including jungle species and imported durian), jias, perah, kulim
   - Fruiting trees used by hunters were damaged by tree felling and machinery

4. **Natural resources destroyed due to extraction of timber by heavy machinery:**
   - Herbal medicines such as *manaar* (pakma), *kacíp* and *tɛnruul* (toŋkat ali) are lost in some areas once rich with them
   - Edible plants are now hard to find or growth is reduced due to pollution of machinery oil
   - Bamboo has been devastated in some places
   - Bertam roofing palms devastated by heavy machinery on the hill-sides and caused to die off due to lack of natural shade from the sun
   - Rivers full of logging debris will take ten years or more to clear out
   - Waterfalls and places of natural beauty have been bulldozed, e.g. Tɛŋkơh Ləruw, where a temporary bridge was made and rocks bulldozed aside
   - Ipoh trees (blow-dart poison tree) damaged or cut down for timber

5. **The forest ecosystem has been irreversibly damaged or lost:**
   - Wild animals have left the logging areas (deer, primates, birds, rodents)
   - Thousands of plant species lost, possibly many endemic in this part of Kelantan
   - Piped water supply full of mud and sand and often cuts off after rain
   - Dozens of land-slides, soil erosion causing lack of growth of natural species
   - Fish are depleted in the rivers due to sanding, once deep pools are now shallow

6. **Logging activities cause many disturbances to villagers:**
   - Daily noise and danger of machinery at logging yards and trucks passing village homes
   - Areas under operation are unsafe for villagers, they must stay out
   - Areas after operation are a tangle of destruction and the original jungle paths have been destroyed
   - These temporary roads soon become gutted by rain water run-off and collapse in deep holes.

10.4   THE TEMIARS' RESPONSE TO TWENTY YEARS OF LOGGING

Resisting the logging companies has been difficult for the Temiars. They are not accustomed to making confrontations, especially with the Chinese, Malay and foreign workers who have been active in the region. Many of the loggers threatened violence if resistance was met. Other times they came with gifts of food and promises that they wouldn't take too much timber. In the early years the Temiars didn't know how to take action and confront the loggers and by the time a network of villages had been formed in Kelantan, so much irreversible damage had already been made. After 2010, the Temiars began to reach out to the government, submitting several memorandums to state their plight and their traditional rights to the land and its resources. Yet it seemed as if the state was refusing to open any dialogue with the Temiar community, the senior minister was always 'out' or 'busy' when delegations were sent up to Kota Bharu with letters, desiring to have a meeting.

With all other avenues exhausted, they began to feel that the only option they had was to halt the destruction of their forest themselves, by blockading the access roads. The communities of Gɔɔb, Símpor, Pasíg and Bihay coordinated and built blockades (some four efforts in five years), that managed to prevent all logging activities in their customary land, sometimes for months on end.

In December, 2011, a protest was made at Putra Jaya, involving a large number of Temiars from Kelantan. This was followed by a protest in January, 2012, at Kampuŋ Paríᵏ, near Kuala Betis, involving two hundred men, women and children. They waved hundreds of placards with messages of discontent about the extensive logging and commercial operations on Orang Asli ancestral land. The protest was led by the late Taaᵏ ʔAro̱m, of Pos Bihay, and Jaringan Kampung Orang Asli Kelantan (or JKOAK, the network of Orang Asli villages in kelantan). It didn't last longer than a few days, as the police soon arrested the ring-leaders and carted them off to Gua Musang in a lorry, for a night in the lockup.

Protesters at the Temiars' first blockade, in 2012, which caused quite a stir.

In April, 2016, the second blockade was made and this time at Pos Gɔɔb itself, as the villagers became desperate to halt or pause the felling of prime forest on all the hills around. The effort was led by the leaders of the community and they first handed notice of their demands to halt all logging activities to the bosses at the logging yard. Once the blockade was up they faced almost daily visits from Forestry officials, who drove up in small numbers to try to persuade the barricaders to lift the barrier. Offerings of food and tobacco were dumped on the ground by the logging bosses, thinking that they could buy them off cheaply. It was eventually opened up after a month-long stand, but it did manage to disrupt the logging, if only for a short while. It was also the first time that the Temiars of Pos Gɔɔb had voiced their displeasure and made demands based on their rights as the indigenous population in the land. The Temiars at the Píɲcơˀoŋ River also made demands to the loggers working at the Ləruw waterfall, who were causing the Píɲcơˀoŋ to flow with murky water, but they were unable to keep a blockade on the road going up there

Temiars meet with the logging boss at the Rơndoŋ logging yard, in 2016, to demand an immediate cessation of logging activities in their forest. (Credit: Yusman ˀAndoᵏ)

Temiars meet at the late ˀUda Siyam's home to discuss taking action to halt the logging.

Temiars man a blockade at Kacəŋ, 200m from Pos Gɔɔb, in an attempt to halt the logging operations in 2015. (Credit, 3 pictures: various)

Officials from the timber association and forestry department, along with logging bosses and the police, listen to a statement read by the Temiars manning a blockade at Gɔɔb.

In September of 2016, the third effort began, and this time it was combined with the Pos Símpor and Pos Pasíg communities. It was staged down at the tip of the territories of the above named, at a hill-top known to them as TaŋkoꞋl LaŋoꞋy (Communist Hill), on the road from Kuala Betis. The blockade practically became a small Temiar village, with a shelter for each participating community and a meeting hall. Various NGOs assisted the Temiars (on humanitarian grounds) by sponsoring foodstuff, as there was no way that the Temiars could bring enough food from home or find it around the camp, which was surrounded by deforested and terraced land. The blockade was broken down after a few months' standing, on a rainy day in December, by the Forestry department, arriving in twenty vehicles and using chainsaws. Some 54 persons were arrested during the proceedings and taken to Gua Musang town, and held for a night at the lockup (with the police this time unwilling to cooperate with the Forestry Dept) and also over a dozen motorbikes were carted away (and were held for months).

In February, 2017, the same blockade was rebuilt at LaŋoꞋy Hill, but subsequently it was destroyed by bulldozer, soon after. The blockade put a halt to the rampant forest clearance that had gone on throughout 2016 until then, of the Waaj River area and around the TꞋhoꞋr pass. It also halted logging activities on the Upper Puyan and PíɲcoꞋŋ, giving the villagers some breathing space. The effort was not limited to the area of Pos GoꞋb and Pos Símpor alone as blockades were also built on the two roads to Pos Bihay and Pos Pasíg at the same time.

The blockade at LaŋoꞋy Hill, which became a small village in itself.

Map of the Puyan, drawn by the Pos Gɔɔb community, demonstrating their knowledge of the land.

Logging companies removed all their machinery from the area.

Authorities arrived in force and dismantled the Temiars' blockade, in 2017. (Credit, 5 pictures: various)

A year later, in <u>2018</u>, the fourth effort was made, and this time on the road from Kuala Betis, at a point near Guwɔɔᵏ Cɔɔs (the historic Gua Cha). Initially the blockade managed in force the removal of logging machinery but it soon received much attention by bosses and workers of a certain company that had already opened up a durian estate on Pos Símpor land (some 300 ha.). Being frustrated that they were denied access to their plantation, they persisted and bickered, and even threw verbal abuse at the Temiars manning the barricade. One day saw the plantation workers bring along their security guards, holding weapons at their side to intimidate. The blockade was broken down several times, once by a hired gang from B'tɨs, using chainsaws, and once by the Forestry Department, on quite a grand scale. Since then the blockades have not continued, but the result of the last effort was that Putra Jaya (the Federal government) heard the voice of the Temiars and showed sympathy toward their situation.

The 2018 blockade at the Kalox River, near the historic rock shelter of Guwɔɔᵏ Cɔɔs.

Deputy Minister for Rural Development, Sivarasa Rasiah, pays a visit o the Temiar blockade.

Workers from the durian plantation bring armed security guards with them to intimidate the Temiars holding the blockade. (Credit, 4 pictures: various)

During the protests, another group of Temiars emerged to voice their opinions, the anti-protest and pro-land development faction. They argued that the actions of JKOAK were only creating disharmony between the government and the OA community, stating that the government has been the one feeding them and giving free care services these last fifty years. They descended on the blockades several times, to try and disrupt the effort and force them to open the barricade for the loggers and durian plantation workers. Among them were ˀAbu ˀAlɔŋ (son of the late Pəŋhuluᵏ ˀAlɔŋ ˀAlʉj of R'koʊ̌b, mentioned on p120), Pəŋhuluᵏ Liman ˀAlaŋ of Pos Gɔɔb, Pəŋhuluᵏ Zainal of Pos Tohoʏ, Pəŋhuluᵏ ˀAsím ˀAlɔŋ of Pos Pasíg, ˀAgooh Tɛˀɛŋ of Kampuŋ Wʉʉd, Pəŋhuluᵏ Jumat ˀAbaᵏ of Kampuŋ Lamboᵏ, Latif Siyam of Kampuŋ T'ranɛᵏ and ˀAlɔŋ ˀAroᵏ of Kampuŋ Jiyas (Lamboᵏ, T'ranɛᵏ and Jiyas are all near B'tʉs). There were others who voiced opposition to the demonstrations, from Pos B'roʊ̌x, Pos Haw, Pos Bəər, Pos Hɛnrəb and Tuwɛl, whose names I don't have, but these eight persons mentioned were certainly the most vocal.

They made simple and short-sighted claims, such as that life would be difficult if the roads deteriorated, due to lack of repairs made by logging companies, while failing to see what a huge environmental impact the companies make wherever they build those roads. Hills and mountains are stripped of forest and soil erosion, land-slides, river silting and disappearance of wild animals become common place. Perhaps 90% of the community, bar these village chiefs just mentioned, who gloat lavish pay-offs for themselves, still depend on the the unspoiled forest for maintaining their livelihoods. It is stated by JKOAK representatives that with the rivers turned red with soil wash-off and the complete disappearance of fish that were once easy to catch (especially at the B'roʊ̌x River), it is impossible to side with the claims of the *pɛmbaŋkaŋ*, or anti-protest faction, the only ones claiming that mass redevelopment of the land carries true benefit for the Temiar community.

10.2 In any other context, the Malay word 'asli' actually means original, as in genuine, and thus the term, Orang Asli, should literally mean 'original' or 'real' man. It also carries no implication of belonging to the land, leading to some indigenous groups to now call themselves Orang Asal, or 'originating people' to show that they are native to the land.

In truth, the 'disharmony' they speak against is the voice of a people being heard. Their land is being sold off, with some dire results for the inhabitants who depend on it. The desires of the indigenous community clash, unsurprisingly, with the aspirations of the wealthy, who, in the Temiars' mind, are *galag*, or greedy, and are not content with the space they have in their own land, and this is what boils down to a discord. In over sixty years since Malaysia's independence, barely any ancestral lands of the Orang Asli[2] (none at all for the Kelantan Temiars) have been gazetted as OA reserve land. The native inhabitants are still forced to prove in court that their ancestors were resident in their territories and that they continue to depend on the land for their livelihood, in order to safeguard it from permanent and irreversible re-management. And these court cases can take ten years or more to reach a verdict, which may not even favour them in the end. All the while, they have to fight their case as if they were foreigners, with the state siding with the wealthy corporations.

11 | THE PUYAN TEMIARS IN THE PRESENT DAY

11.1   THE TEMIARS AND THEIR LAND

Until the present day, the soul of the Puyan Temiars is intimately woven with the land of their forefathers, through the souls of their ancestors who first roamed and planted in it, and to take them from the land (as happened before) or to take the land from them (which is constantly feared) is to cut off the life of their soul. It seems that the indigenous people are expected to adapt over night and look for other occupations and food sources, but without their roots intact it can only lead to their distress. Not only do they feel that the land is sacred and should be guarded forever from harm, but they know that their age-old way of life is becoming threatened. They continue to visit the hills where the loggers have not yet reached, to hunt and forage, but these areas are now a long walk from the village, and most of the vital resources are now impossible to find nearby.

Although community life has changed somewhat over the last fifty years, and especially in the last twenty years since villages have become more permanently settled, there is still a desire and a need to roam about the land. They especially need to cut new swiddens where crops will grow well and produce food to support their families. The many l'mog, or former sites which their ancestors cultivated a hundred or more years ago are still being re-used and re-cultivated, due to the fact that they are well situated, with good soil and near to rivers. Not all are replanted, of course, but many of them are frequented by the Temiars to collect from the dozens of fruit trees that have grown into forest. As of 2021, the Tɛmagaaᵏ and Bɘrcaap villagers tend a few swiddens along the Bɘrtax cut at places that Taaᵏ K'lusar had also re-used, such as S'rijơơh (one of the oldest settlements of the Puyan Temiar), Lagoh, and Labuᵏ.

The Temiars of Gɔɔb and B'rơg villages maintain a swidden a day's walk up the Puyan, at Capɛɛr, and Temiars of Pinaŋ village plant swiddens up the Píɲcơơŋ River valley. Most of these places are several hour's walk from the villages they now consider home, proving that they need much more than a few small plots of land to live off.[1] The same is true for them as it was for their ancestors a hundred years ago, that once an area of land has been cut and planted for a number of years, they need to move on and find land that has been left to itself and returned to forest. The majority of Temiars in the Puyan valley still consider themselves the guardians of the land, and by roaming and planting swiddens they maintain a year-on-year watch over it, as far as the water-shed boundaries. Their many forest camps in the upriver areas, are constantly accessed by groups of hunters, who feel just as much at home sleeping on the ground, under leafy roofs, as they do at the village with its water pipes and and motor traffic.

The loggers claim that the road they built, with its treacherous mud holes and collapsing log bridges, is a great gift to the Orang Asli and they should be thankful for it. But life was arguably better before the road reached the villages and they enjoyed a degree of security in their isolation. Lone, unfamiliar cars are suspected of carrying *CB*, or child abductors (from the Malay, colek budak), and

11.1 Some years back, JAKOA was proposing to alot each household two acres of land to live on, with the rest leased for development (sukad tɛᵏ, in the Temiars' own words, divide the land). At the same time, if the scheme was implemented, villagers would lose all rights to the land outside their designated boxes, so that ultimately they could be fined for foraging and collecting forest products in the land that has been theirs to freely roam for many generations.

reports frequently circulate of persons disappearing or having been attacked by machete-wielding men. Pakistani traders, who have been riding in by motorbike for the last ten years, selling clothes, hair-clips, ice creams and portable stereos, often act suspiciously, as if looking for someone to snatch. One of them grabbed a child at Tɛmagaaᵏ village, but was chased off.

Parents are ever fearful that their children could disappear one day—as happened to the child of Tuŋal ˀAlʉj of Rʹkoʹob village, near Pos Simpor, back in 2000. The mother had left her child sleeping in a sling and went to collect something at the nearby swidden. It was during the time of logging operations in the Símpor region and that day, in her absence, a group arrived by car and they saw the child in the sling and took it. In recent years, the boy has made contact with his real family, but he hasn't returned to them. The only useful change that the dirt road has brought in is trading, but the producers are left to scrape a living from the meager prices set for them.

By observing the Temiars today, one would think that their life-style has shifted to closer dependence on town commodities, such as rice, oil and sugar, and that as a result they have let go of the traditional ways that were kept by former generations. But the shifting dependence is actually a forced effect of the diminishing resources around them and is proportional to the amount of damage and removal of forest that their traditional ways depended on. The Temiars of old were hard-working, and they had to build, gather, hunt, tie traps, climb trees, medicate illnesses, and above all find food for each day.

The obtaining of rice seed in the 1960s brought a welcome change of life-style by providing up to ten to twelve months of food from each year's crop. It was also easier to store and prepare than the millet they had lived on previously, and it could be planted in the hotter, low-land valleys. Together with their hunting, fishing and gathering they had a period of plenty, for forty years or so. And then came the logging companies, with gangs electrocuting and bombing river pools. By 2010, elephants began encroaching on village swiddens, stamping on the rice fields and pulling up the manioc.

A good rice harvest in 2018 gave sackfuls of grain, but it was the last successful planting to date, and potentially the last ever if the seed runs out, which is from the 1960s.

Long ago, elephants that inhabited the highlands survived off wild banana trees and bamboo shoots and they were timid, rarely ever encroaching on human-settled areas. Now they seem to live off the swiddens of the Temiars, as if the people were responsible for feeding them, and are often angry when met. Lorries have been seen dropping off elephants on the road, to send them 'back into the wild', but these are actually finding their way back to Temiar villages to cause havoc. In the last five years, the mud-brown tuskers have been responsible for crop destruction in a dozen villages, from S'daal, Jadεεr and P'naad, to Gawíín, Jərnεy, Tanjuŋ, Kajaax, Pɪ́ɲcʊ́ʊŋ, Bərcaap, Tεmagaaᵏ and B'rɤ́g. Fortunately, no one in this region has been attacked or injured.

An elephant stomping on the rice field, at Pɪ́ɲcʊ́ʊŋ.

Destruction of a manioc patch, in 2019.

When they find no more banana trees to knock down or patches of manioc to uproot, they then start getting angry and pulling down houses to search for bags of salt and bottles of oil. To protect their homes, villagers often need to stay up all night, shining torches and beating on oil cans. Only two animals were removed by the authorities, from around Kampuŋ Jadεεr, in 2019. If the Temiars take action they risk being fined or jailed, as happened at Pos Pasíg in the same year, when an elephant was shot (it had become extremely dangerous) and the man who shot it was jailed for three months. The elephants trample the rice fields as they are sprouting, causing the crop to fail, or as the crop ripens (as in 2022), creating severe food shortages and hunger for villagers.

During the floods of 2014, when it rained incessantly for weeks on end, there were large land-slips all up the Puyan where logging had caused instability, and whole manioc fields were washed away. Now the rivers have sanded up and catching fish requires skill, luck and hours of throwing a casting net, because the fish are often swept away by flash flooding.

The Kacəŋ River in flood, once a clean water source for the villagers of Gɔɔb. Only since rampant logging took place in the water catchment has this began to occur. (Credit: Yusman ʔAndoⁱᵏ)

A boy casts a net on the water of the Puyan River.

A typical catch of fish using today's method of casting a chain-weighted net, as bigger fish tend to hide in rock holes.

Nasir Samsudin, of Píɲcoʼoŋ, holds a large Mahseer carp, quite an unusual catch these days due to the scarcity of fish in the last twenty years.

All these effects have pushed the Temiars toward a low level of peasantry, turning their efforts toward making light cash in order to buy town-made commodities they now need to live on. In the early days, there was *mano͞w* rattan to cut and sell, which is used in the furniture trade. Then that was depleted and they turned to collecting herbal roots like *kacíp* (*Labisia pumila*) and *tɛnruul* (*Euycoma longifolia*; Malay, tongkat ali), and fruits such as *so͞ic* and *ʔaŋgru*y (Malay, keranji), for Malay consumption, or export to Thailand. In recent years, traders have been paying higher prices for durians, giving up to RM4 per kilogramme, instead of RM1 or less per fruit, as in previous years. But it still depends on the market and the traders themselves, whether they cheat or not.

In the last five or six years, bananas have been planted en mass, but the price remains very low. In 2018, the banana trees succumbed to a blight that rotted the fruits and although they have recovered, traders have been few in 2020-2021. The price of rubber is also too low at Gɔɔb to warrant the labour to tap the trees. On top of that, some traders use 'locked' weighing scales, that don't depress fully, and producers sometimes receive only RM6 (US$1.50) for two large bunches, and might make only around RM24 per week! In the 1990s, traders sought after *g'haru*ᵏ, the fragrant agarwood, from which they made millions, but the Temiars never saw much reward from what they sourced, as they were either told that the quality was too low or that the price had gone down. Following that, Thais and Cambodians on tourist visas wandered the forests extracting all that remained of the resinous wood. They showed up once at a village, looking for food, unable to speak Malay and carrying guns, which disturbed the Temiars.

Kacíp roots, a herb used in post-natal care, are chopped up and dried in the sun before sale. (Credit: ʔAnɛl)

ʔAŋgruy, a fruit of a bean pod that makes bean sprouts which are popular in Thailand.

Kɛsmas (Malay, susu harimau), a fungus that is used in herbal medicine and can be sold for cash.

Some members of the community do not seek to preserve their ancestral land, however, or even their own customs, but are willing to trade off everything they can for personal gains. The headman of Pos Gɔɔb, Liman ʔAlaŋ, is the most notable example. In 2016, he and his close relatives negotiated a pickup-truck (after their request for RM2 million was declined) from a logging company, in exchange for consent to extensive logging of the Upper Puyan River area. Consultation with the other headmen of the Puyan valley or with the larger community was completely by-passed. Reportedly, they have recently signed off the entire eastern side of the Puyan valley for oil palm development, the mono-crop said to be "produced from responsible resources". Responsible resources meaning that the palm trees are replanted when they are old, the natural forest is lost forever.

11.2   FORCES CHANGING THE TEMIAR WAY OF LIFE

The most obvious disturbance, heard on some days, is the roar of Air Force fighter jets flying up the valley and then soaring into the deep blue sky, often making sonic booms, that shudder across the mountains. Sometimes it is wondered if the planes are scouring for a target to bomb, such as a village or two, as no one knows where they come from. But besides this irritating noise from above, which often provokes curses from below, there is plenty of interference that finds its way in by four-wheel drive vehicle.

In the last ten years, or perhaps ever since the road opened the way, Pos Gɔɔb has become a hot spot for group excursions from the cities, who camp at the old clinic and landing zone (or rent the new thatch-roof chalets), making all the noise they like. Temiar culture bears little significance with them and is only shown some feigned appreciation. 'Progressive' townspeople descend on the 'backward' kampung dwellers, imposing their own values. The villagers need encouragement, after all, to adapt to the changes around them and catch up with society. Sports and games are put on, with loud karaoke sessions going into the night. Hot food is dished out and cash gifts put in hands. Islamic volunteers roll in to *kampɛɛn*, or promote their religion, knocking on doors at seven in the morning, before anyone has a chance to leave for the swidden, extracting conversions from those who believe they will become fed and cared for. Only a handful, however, of the villagers at Gɔɔb have *moʔoj ʔalɛl*, 'converted to the reciters of Arabic', to date.

For most Temiars, there is no need to adopt any new world religion, with its foreign deities and no freedom to opt out of later. They certainly do not see religion in the same light as the agencies trying to assimilate them do. To the Temiars, their ancestry and tradition form who they are ethnically, and even if they adopt a religion, they are still Temiar at heart, with their belief in souls of the wild and the need for soul-mediumship. But to the pushers of religion, it is perceived that adoption of their ideology means leaving behind the old traditions and even a person's ethnic identity.

A fair number of NGOs have been at Pos Gɔɔb in the last ten years, either bringing food aid or looking for projects to run that would garner funding. Contractors also, who seldom hold any discourse with the villagers, to learn what real needs exist, or what developments people would consent to. Plans are drawn up in a town office and something flimsy is built (such as the water taps, installed in 2019, that became fountains after a week) and the ideas of the locals are ignored. The villagers have to stand by and watch what happens and when the builders leave the apparatus is often left to rust.

Government aid reaches the villages from time to time, with the most notable being a subsidy housing scheme, called PPRT. The scheme provides a dinky, tin roof home for each applicant family, with walls and floors

Subsidy homes at Pos Gɔɔb. (Credit: Johan ʔAlɨj)

that crack, due to shortcuts taken in spending. These homes were built at Lʼhɛɛŋ and Kacəŋ, near the clinic at Pos Gɔɔb, in the years 2014-2018. Since then the scheme seems to have stalled, as there are still nine villages without permanent homes built, while natural building materials are becoming increasingly difficult to source. Not that the villagers are really happy with a breakable cement home which they can't repair themselves, or remove when it has crumbled, as most would prefer wooden planked homes (as were provided thirty years ago in some places like Pos Símpor). A great help would be to provide the tin roofing and let them build their own homes.

A water treatment pump station in disuse. (Credit: Johan ʔalʉj)

Rolls of pipes are delivered for installing in a gravity water system. (Credit: ʔAnɛl)

Another subsidy, is the provision of durable water pipes, that are laid to supply water by gravity from a higher river source. Without these in place the only option would be fetching water by plastic bottle from a nearby river or stream. What the villages didn't need however was the multi-million dollar installation of UV water treatment systems, powered by noisy diesel engines. Since these were installed in 2009, at every Temiar village, none of them have been operational or have delivered in the goal of providing clean water. The water pipes are often refitted to bypass the system, so that the disused storage tanks don't become frog sanctuaries or silt up with mud. It would have cost only RM60 per household to provide clean drinking water, using commercially available gravity filters. Probably less than 1% of the water supply is used for consumption anyway, with the open pipe ends gushing out water all day and night. In some areas, the mountain water is perfectly safe to drink without treatment and it only turns murky for a while after the rain.

In the last few years, from 2018-2020, the Health Ministry have provided monthly visits to the villages by car, replacing the air-borne visits that took place before that. These visits have been more intrusive on the lifestyle of the Temiars, as, instead of allowing the villagers to come at their own leisure, for check-ups and medicines, the medical team roll in with four or five cars, right to their doorsteps. They also voice displeasure if villagers are absent during the visit, not considering that foraging in the surrounding valley is an essential part of every day survival.

A flying doctor helicopter lands at Kajaaᵏ, in 2016. (Credit, two pictures: ²Anεl)

A Health Ministry visit in progress.

Expectant mothers are registered and given an ultrasound scan. Home births are discouraged, although not completely forbidden, even though most women would be more comfortable giving birth at home. They are told that home births are high-risk, while the hospital is safer, but some locals argue that there is also a risk giving birth at hospital, noting the case of a woman from B'rod, in 2016, who after safely giving birth was later pronounced deceased. In any case, there are a hundred hurdles created for registration of children born at home, and thus many parents have the birth at town, so that the process will be made easier for them.

The insistence on hospital births has, unfortunately, led to the demise of midwifery among the Temiars. Experienced midwifes, who are mostly of the older generation, are no longer passing on their vital knowledge to younger women. Not only do their skills seem unneeded these days, but they are also afraid to assist a birth and then later on be investigated by the nurses. It may also create dangers because the villages are still a long way from town, and are sometimes cut off by a fallen bridge or bad weather, and in an emergency situation a doctor may not be able to fly in and assist. One such emergency happened at Gawíin village in 2020, resulting in the loss of the mother, and the doctor flew in only to note the cause of death.

Infants receive post-natal checkups, with their follow-up jabs, which, they say, will make them healthier. But parents say there are often unwanted side-effects, such as body rashes and high temperature, which worry them considerably. Family planning is eagerly carried out with mothers of children, by the insertion of contraceptive implants in their arms (called in Malay, perancang) or by an injection (perancang susu). These are known by Temiar women to cause uncomfortable side-effects, such as migraines and obesity, in the case of the implant, and swelling of the waist, in the case of the injection. Once removed or worn off, they can also cause a woman to miscarry or have complications giving birth.

And here is the clash of two worlds, as modern medicine meets with a deeply rooted dependence on traditional remedies, for little is known about the Temiars' knowledge of medicinal practice. The herbs they use in daily preparations have never been catalogued or tested (refer to my Chapter 5 for a first attempt!), which make a vital part of their own health system, the one they prefer by far. Temiar villages are considered fairly disease-prone places, in need of outside assistance in order to avert health crises. Whereas, in reality, the Temiars are possibly of better health than other people groups, due to their existence away from pollution, their daily consumption of organic foods and their freedom to walk in the green environment around them. The visiting nurses look at the village women and assess them as being malnourished, unaware that food is sometimes hard to come by. But even the doctor from Ipoh remarked a few years ago that the villagers were in good physical condition.

The main health concerns facing the Temiars, excluding jungle-born illnesses, which, it is believed, modern medicines cannot help, are scabies, fungal skin infections and intestinal worm infestations, with cases of tuberculosis and malaria being extremely rare. I have seen at least two cases of prolonged untreated cases of intestinal worms in children, causing them to became literally skin and bones. After a simple worms treatment and daily vitamins and healthy food they were both able to recover over a period of six months, but one of the girls developed epilepsy as a possible result (since cured after further worm treatment). There are several known cases of epilepsy in the villages here, but the visiting doctors have never found out about them. Epileptic seizures are perceived as resulting from consumption of tabooed animals during childhood and therefore the condition would likely not be reported.

At hospital, new-born babies are kept under observation for up to a month, and the family have to stay at the adjacent hostel, sitting on the floor doing nothing all that time. Because they are transported to hospital sometimes a month before the delivery, they can be held there for up to two months, which seems an excruciating long time for people who have many chores to attend (missed time at the swidden could mean a lack of food in the near future). The Temiars say that they never had problems with 'yellow babies' in the past, not before so many processed foods entered their diet. But these days they know of the herbal remedies that can alleviate the condition, and some parents just set off for home, to take care of their child themselves.

As part of the anti-malaria programme, village homes are sprayed with pesticide on the walls once or twice a year (ironically causing an increase of mosquitoes, residents say) and mosquito nets are dispensed, being first dipped in the chemical (deltamethrin). The next day sees all the nets hanging out to dry after washing, because to sleep under them after the dipping causes health problems. The people spraying the walls tell them that it's harmless, while at the same time warning them not to let children touch anything that was sprayed! Blood samples are also taken from as many people as are still wiling to give their finger for a prick, but many feel that they are being accused as the source of diseases in the country.

In 2015, University Malaysia Sarawak (UniMas) came along and built an internet centre at Pos Gɔɔb, undertaking only minimal research beforehand as to how this might affect the community. As it turned out, the villagers had no real application for the new service, with no actual goals put in place and no ventures started (such as running businesses or tourism) and no one had any prior experience with the internet. While communications among the Orang Asli may have been improved, at the same time the centre became a hot-spot for video downloading (adult content and pop music), causing a major disruption to normal Temiar culture and society. In 2021, someone took an axe to the router due to his frustration that the women folk were constantly messaging and neglecting their daily chores!

Twenty years of interference by a Chinese Christian group, called Gospel To The Poor (GTTP), has had no real benefit either for the few villages that have entertained them for so long. Their key strategy to keeping a foothold in the region has been with free food each week and a monthly salary for each village headman. The pastors condemn those who defer from attending meetings, branding them sinners with no hope. Later, they try to win them back after realising that they need the numbers! The group bans wearing of head bands by men and the adorning with flowers by women, as well as holding any form of the traditional dance, saying that such practices are demonic. Traditional funerals are no longer allowed and when I went to attend the soul-sending ceremony of the late Pəŋhuluᵏ P′diᵏ, I was shocked to see a large group of Chinese turning the event into a party, sharing out fizzy drinks and cheap snacks. The attitude of the Chinese pastors, who can be hot-tempered at times, as they squash people down for any small mistake, is in complete contrast to the Temiars' passive and patient culture. The lack of genuine care for the Temiars shows clearly that they are only here for financial gains (to be made from donations).

I had a conversation, once, with one of the Chinese regulars, Ah Yee, a former logger who lived at Jadɛɛr village in the '90s. According to the locals, his life was saved by the Temiars at Laloᵏ, the place of the Temiar prophet of the 1990s, when he was left behind in the forest by his fellow comrades and was starving with hunger. From his response, it was clear that he held his own culture as far superior to the Temiars'. I asked him why, after all those years of continual visits, they hadn't taught any children to read or write and he replied that the Temiars can't learn anything. The only way would be to take them out of their home environment, while young, and put into mainstream schooling at town. In other words, to remove their culture from them. This GTTP has been doing for the last five years, putting children in Chinese schools, and they have been coming home at the end of the year speaking languages that their parents can't understand. Their parents have been led to look down on their own culture and living conditions, so as to pack up their children and send them off, without knowing where they are going.

Another group, Tribal Ministry, from Malacca, has been gathering children from the Temiars since 2018, and they seem quite happy that the Temiars are embracing new ideology and leaving their traditions. I mentioned to the pastor how the environment around is still threatened, and he replied, "They can't be naturalists forever!" And, "God is changing the Temiars!" But is it not really their own extravagance, arriving with their monster trucks loaded to the roof with food and gifts, that is creating the culture shift? Not to mention that when a stout male shakes hands with the women, it causes them to laugh and flirt all the while, as if caught by a love spell. Their actions have also caused much division among the community, as each group clings to their own NGO, and hoards the food aid for themselves, unwilling to share it with those who won't join them.

Village children are creative: boys make wooden cars and girls play with stick dolls.

One young boy from Tɛmagaaᵏ who has now been schooled in the city a number of years.

Play houses are made from manioc leaf stems.

Many young people have been lost to town from the villages, as they join friends who have already found jobs (minimal paid factory jobs usually) and are naive of the dangers. Taking young children away, as they are doing, may add to the statistic of urban Temiars in the end, at a time when the community needs people to reside at home and live the Temiar life, to demonstrate that the land is owned and their history and traditions are still alive.

Two girls at Kacəŋ wash vegetables in clean-flowing mountain water and a boy at Tanjuŋ wears an elaborate headdress, in preparation for a dance.

APPENDIX 2

List Of Place Names In The Pos Gɔɔb Territory

The list here contains over 1000 primary names gathered from the territory of Pos Gɔɔb (out of 1650 places that were surveyed over a five year period, from 2013-2018), categorised into types of name origin. The table below shows the total numbers of names allocated to each category of name origin for each geographic place type. Refer to Part 6.2 for a more detailed description.

Some names appear to have duplicates and this is because certain places have been named after the same species of tree, flower, plant, animal, or, in some cases, the same environmental condition, event or dream. These duplicate names may count for 100 or more names from the total. A number in parenthesis indicates multiple occurrences of the same name.

Category Name / Place Type (Total)	Tree	Hunter's tree	Fruit	Plant	Medicinal	Flower	Vine	Bamboo	Tiger	Animal	Bird	Insect	Environment	Weather	Event	Feeling	Person	Man-made	Crop	Food	Custom	Spiritual	Catastrophe	Death	Dream
	Plant Species								Animal Species						Human Factors							Non-Human			
Swidden (l'mog) (133)	20	17	13	5	2	6	4	4	5	4	7	4	10	2	8	-	4	4	5	2	2	2	2	-	1
	71								19				12		26							5			
Mountain (jɛlmɤl) (131)	22	6	1	9	5	12	3	4	2	3	1	1	18	6	8	5	4	1	-	2	1	-	-	-	17
	62								7				24		21							17			
Hill (taŋkɤl) (221)	55	33	19	14	7	7	9	6	4	12	3	2	13	4	12	1	3	2	2	2	1	1	1	-	8
	150								21				17		23							10			
Gully (luwag) (75)	17	3	4	9	5	4	1	1	3	5	1	2	3	-	3	1	3	3	1	2	1	1	-	-	2
	44								11				3		14							3			
Ridge (gɛrbɔɔᵏ) (41)	7	5	1	3	2	1	1	2	-	1	5	1	4	1	4	1	-	-	-	-	-	1	-	1	-
	22								7				5		5							2			
Boulder (batuᵏ) (17)	1	-	-	2	-	-	1	1	-	1	-	-	4	1	3	1	-	-	-	-	-	-	-	-	2
	5								1				5		4							2			
Cave (guwɔɔᵏ) (13)	1	-	-	-	-	1	-	-	-	2	1	-	1	-	3	-	1	2	-	-	-	1	-	-	-
	2								3				1		6							1			
Valley (l'gəp) (3)	1	1	-	-	-	-	-	-	-	-	-	-	-	-	-	-	-	-	-	-	-	-	-	-	1
	2								-				-		-							1			
River (ʔoɤx) (221)	30	26	9	27	3	7	4	5	7	23	5	11	23	2	16	2	2	4	-	3	4	-	-	-	8
	111								46				25		31							8			
Waterfall (tɛŋkɤh) (46)	8	4	1	4	1	2	-	-	-	5	-	-	15	1	-	-	1	2	-	-	-	1	-	1	-
	20								5				16		3							2			
River pool (gool) (80)	23	15	6	7	1	-	1	5	-	7	-	-	6	-	2	-	4	2	-	1	-	-	-	-	-
	58								7				6		9							-			
Island (rapag) Cliff (ʔamparr)	-	-	-	2	-	-	-	-	-	-	1	1	-	-	-	-	-	-	-	-	-	-	-	-	-
	2								2				-		-							-			

Place Type (Total)	Plant Species								Animal Species				Environment	Weather	Human Factors							Non-Human			
	Tree	Hunter's tree	Fruit	Plant	Medicinal	Flower	Vine	Bamboo	Tiger	Animal	Bird	Insect	Environment	Weather	Event	Feeling	Person	Man-made	Crop	Food	Custom	Spiritual	Catastrophe	Death	Dream
Inland pool (cagool) (2)	-	-	-	-	-	-	-	-	-	-	-	-	1	-	-	-	-	-	-	-	-	-	1	-	-
(subtotals)				-							-		1					-					1		
Bog (l'baax) (5)	-	-	-	-	-	1	-	-	-	-	-	-	2	-	-	-	-	-	-	-	-	-	2	-	-
(subtotals)				1							-		2					-					2		
Spring (j'nood) (1)	-	-	-	-	-	-	-	-	-	-	-	-	1	-	-	-	-	-	-	-	-	-	-	-	-
(subtotals)				-							-		1					-					-		
Tree (j'huuk) (9)	-	-	-	-	-	-	-	-	1	-	1	-	1	-	1	-	1	1	-	-	1	1	-	-	1
(subtotals)				-							2		1					4					2		
Army landing point (LP) (3)	-	-	-	-	-	-	-	-	1	-	-	-	-	-	-	-	1	-	-	-	-	-	-	-	1
(subtotals)				-							1		-					1					1		
Category Totals	185	110	54	82	26	41	24	28	22	63	25	22	102	17	61	11	24	21	8	12	10	8	6	2	42
Totals (1005)	550								133				119		146							58			
Total (%)	54.7								13.2				11.9		14.5							5.7			

Table 8. Total names of each category for each geographic place.

GROUP 1: NATURAL SPECIES I

The names in Group 1 are all names of species, except those marked by an *, which have explanatory notes below them. Some names in the plant column also carry explanation alongside them,

Forest Trees	Hunters' Trees	Fruit Trees	Plants	
Swidden (l'mog)				
B'luŋɛy	Canul	Bagan	ˀAbən	from gantən, zingiber sp.
Calyɛx	Guwaaɲ (2)	Calɛɛr*	Karas	=j'rox, palm sp.
Cəlˀɛl	J'riyɛw	Jɛnɛɛs	Lamog	from lambog, yam plants
Kalaŋ	Kijɛl	Kərbaah*	Pakuᵏ	edible fern sp.
Kalox	K'jox Jarum*	Kɛnrəd	Sˀˀɛɛb	grass sp.
Katɨᵏ	Nyoy	K'síj		
K'jɛɛr	P'laceᵏ	Pinaŋ		
K'jɛl	P'rigoy	Rambɛy		
K'maraaᵏ*	Saɲyal	Riŋud		
K'rox	Sɛmpaaᵏ*	S'pooy		
Manuŋ	Sɛntɛb	Tampuy		
M'nakan*	Siyaduh*			
Pulɛy (2)	S'lɛjmɛj			
Rumpay	S'lɛmnam			

Forest Trees	Hunters' Trees	Fruit Trees	Plants
Swidden (l'moɡ) – *Continued*			
S'daal	S'maliyɛx		
S'nuŋ	Tajɑɑr		
Tagat	Tapoŋ		
Tagɛɛs	Tihɔɔᵏ		
Tɛrsaaŋ			

K'maraaᵏ : a species of palm tree, also known as *paku pakís*.
M'nakan : a species of jungle durian, otherwise known as *bagan*.
K'jɵx Jarum : A fallen *k'jɵx* tree sprouted and looked like many needles pointing upward; *jarum*, needles.
Sɛmpaaᵏ : *sɛmpaaᵏ* is a generic name for jungle durian varieties.
Siyaduh : *siyaduh* is the name of the durian variety planted here by Taaᵏ K'lusar, around 1970.
Calɛɛr : *k'bəəᵏ calɛɛr* is a fruit tree, similar to *jiyɛɛs* but with smaller fruits.
Kərbaah : *b'rəx kubax* is a fruit tree found here; the name became *kərbaa*.

Mountain (jɛlmɵl)

Forest Trees	Hunters' Trees	Fruit Trees	Plants	
Bakow 1433m	Baay 1370m	Lɛjkuwag 1488m	Bayɛᵏ 1318m	palm sp.
B'sar 1329m	K'rɵx 2026m (2)		Dudùg 1172m	plant sp.
Cabɵl 1705m (2)	Mɛmhiim 1277m		Gərcɛɛŋ 1527m	pandanus sp.
G'maah 1908m	Sɛŋluwac 1112m		Hariyuw 1732m	palm sp.
Gunayuw 1531m	T'rih 1363m		Kamaar 1124m	palm sp.
Hɛmrɛp 1371m			K'rɛnduᵏ 1171m	from *k'ruduᵏ*, plant sp.
J'lax 1224m			K'waar 1448m	palm sp.
K'lacɵᵏ 1040m			S'kɛᵏ 1442m	pandanus sp.
K'mlɛm 1521m			Saŋɛ̄ɛ̄n 1364m	fern sp.
Lɛᵏ 1288m				
Liyɵy 1005m				
Maŋsul 1224m				
Pɛnlaay 1570m				
Rasaw 1684m				
Sakɵb 982m				
Sɛrwəər 1625m (2)				
S'pʉʉh 1798m				
Taraaᵏ 1713m				
T'lɛɛy 1691m (2)				

Hill (taŋkɵl)

Forest Trees	Hunters' Trees	Fruit Trees	Plants	
Bagan 997m	Baay 654m	Biraax 989m (2)	Barʔɵɵb 1002m	fragrant plant sp.
Baloŋ 836m	B'dax 777m	Calaag 313m	Bɛltɵp 737m (2)	palm sp.
Bicɛh 448m (2)	Cɛrmɛɛr 578m	Cɛlpɛl 882m	Bud 620m	edible plant sp.
Bílih 856m	Cintol 213m	D'koh 482m	Haar 520m	pandanus sp.
B'runih 803m	Dulaŋ 779m	J'rɵx 994m	Hariiw 1070m	palm sp.
Cabɵl 562m	G'rutɛɛs 656m	Kabaax 558m	Hɛrpix 472m	from *tapix*, zingiber sp.
Caroh 259m	Jaŋrax 811m	Kərbaah* 634m	Kajaax 356m	pandanus sp.
Caad 452m	J'rɛɛw 1221m	K'laat 479m	Kamaar 1167m	palm sp.
Ciyəd 619m	K'bəəᵏ G'raaw 376m	Nyɛŋ 450m	Koor 630m (2)	palm sp.
Cɵx 435m	K'bəəᵏ Gɛntɵx 538m	Pɛltəl* 364m	K'waar 589m	palm sp.
C'rah 787m	K'jɵx 825m	Rambɛy 364m	P'lɵp 481m	plant sp.
D'rəp 442m	K'lɛŋtɵg 394m	Raɲiiᵏ 394m	Tapix 466m	zingiber sp.
Gapɛh 526m	K'rɛᵏbuᵏ 406m	S'pɵɵy 705m		

Forest Trees	Hunters' Trees	Fruit Trees	Plants
Hill *(taŋkoʼl)* – Continued			

Forest Trees	Hunters' Trees	Fruit Trees	Plants
Gɛjhaij 1081m	Lɛrwɛɛr 788m	Sʼtool 610m	
Gʼsaaᵏ 1001m	Luwaaᵏ 932m	Tampuy 411m	
Hibol 344m	Pacɛy 1041m	Tərlɛŋ 1197m (2)	
Jʼlax 894m	Pahơg 1031m	Wʉʉd 287m	
Jʼrəg 891m (2)	Pʼlacɛᵏ 383m		
Kamíᵏ 1151m	Pʼrɛslís 720m (2)		
Kʼlɛɛr 788m	Rod 283m		
Kʼlɛraaŋ 525m	Rusow 755m (2)		
Kolím 706m	Sagəər 1057m		
Laloᵏ 582m (3)	Sapuŋ* 689m		
Laŋgoᵏ 396m	Siruy 1033m		
Lɛᵏ 1111m (2)	Sʼlamaᵏ* 845m		
Liyɛx 704m	Sʼlɛjmɛj 1106m		
Mancaŋ 934m	Tajɑɑr 896m		
Nɛgsag 1130m	Tanbay 651m		
Palɛy 1160m	Tawaaɲ* 535m		
Pɛlkop 697m	Tawuᵏ 553m		
Pulɛy 1005m (3)	Tʼŋoᵏ 846m		
Raaŋ 346m			
Rʼlap 1188m			
Rompay 293m			
Salɛɛg 841m			
Salɛh 1268m			
Sanyơg 667m			
Sayơj 527m			
Soʼic 586m (2)			
Sugiᵏ 799m			
Tagɛɛs 491m (2)			
Tanaaŋ 798m			
Tɛrmín 560m			
Tʼmusuh 867m			
Wawơh 403m			
Wɛj 411m			

Kamíᵏ   : a large tree swelled in its middle, and this phenomena is called *kambíᵏ*.
Sapuŋ   : the *lʼˀɛɛg* fruit tree is also known as *sapuŋ*.
Sʼlamaᵏ : the *jơơt* fruit tree is also known as *sʼlamaᵏ*.
Tawaaɲ   : from *guwaaɲ*, a fruit tree.
Kərbaah : *bʼrəx kubax* is a fruit tree found here; the name became *kərbaa*.
Pɛltəl   : they were knocking *jiyɛɛs* fruits down, and they were breaking on the ground; *pantəl*, bumping, → *pɛltəl*.

Gully *(luwag)*

Forest Trees	Hunters' Trees	Fruit Trees	Plants
Luwag Bakaw 330m	Luwag Nyɛs 898m	Luwag Jʼrơx 1241m	Luwag Baroᵏ 627m plant sp.
Luwag Bayuur 221m	Luwag Pʼragoᵏ 370m	Luwag Naŋkaaᵏ 1144m	Luwag Bɛltop 1014m palm sp.
Luwag Bʼluɲɛy 221m	Luwag Tɛlbal 1183m	Luwag Pʼloh 512m	Luwag Bơơd Luwag 1516m
Luwag Cox 440m		Luwag Wʉʉd 394m	fragrant plant sp.
Luwag Jʼrəg 514m			Luwag Jarơw 1066m pandanus sp.
Luwag Kʼmíɲam 853m (2)			
Luwag Kʼnalax 854m			
Luwag Lalar 686m			
Luwag Lʼgơơg 442m			

Forest Trees	Hunters' Trees	Fruit Trees	Plants

Gully (luwag) – *Continued*

Forest Trees	Hunters' Trees	Fruit Trees	Plants
Luwag Lɛᵏ 520m			
Luwag Símpor 234m			
Luwag Taŋley 455m			
Luwag Tɛbrob 898m			
Luwag T'lɛɛɣ 1463m			
Luwag T'ramoᵏ 684m			
Luwag Yuyɔr 1338m			

P'loh : *p'loh jiyɛɛ*s are the new fruits of the jias tree, when still small.

Ridge (gɛrbɔɔᵏ)

Forest Trees	Hunters' Trees	Fruit Trees	Plants
Gɛrbɔɔᵏ Cabɔl 447m	Gɛrbɔɔᵏ Jɛrnaŋ 422m	Gɛrbɔɔᵏ Dɛriyan 1010m	Gɛrbɔɔᵏ Bɵʋd 691m fragrant plants
Gɛrbɔɔᵏ Cəŋel 542m	Gɛrbɔɔᵏ J'raŋkoŋ 1006m		Gɛrbɔɔᵏ Kamaar 1274m palm sp.
Gɛrbɔɔᵏ Cɛx 394m	Gɛrbɔɔᵏ K'rɵx 1240m		Gɛrbɔɔᵏ L'bag 804m plant sp.
Gɛrbɔɔᵏ K'miɲam 651m	Gɛrbɔɔᵏ Sɛgsɛg 404m		
Gɛrbɔɔᵏ K'rɵx 394m	Gɛrbɔɔᵏ Yayɛh 744m		
Gɛrbɔɔᵏ M'ŋas 1092m			
Gɛrbɔɔᵏ Tapɛɛɣ 1116m			

Boulder (batuᵏ)

Forest Trees	Hunters' Trees	Fruit Trees	Plants
Batuᵏ B'taar			Batuᵏ Bayíᵏ palm sp.
			Batuᵏ ʔOor from *koor*, palm sp.

Cave (guwɔɔᵏ)

Forest Trees	Hunters' Trees	Fruit Trees	Plants
Guwɔɔᵏ Tadùg			

Valley (l'gəp)

Forest Trees	Hunters' Trees	Fruit Trees	Plants
L'gəp C'rah	L'gəp G'tah		

River (ʔɵʋx)

Forest Trees	Hunters' Trees	Fruit Trees	Plants
ʔɵʋx Caad	ʔɵʋx Bɵt	ʔɵʋx Calaag	ʔɵʋx Barʔɵʋb fragrant plant sp.
ʔɵʋx Capog	ʔɵʋx Gɛrhaar (2)	ʔɵʋx Gayax	ʔɵʋx Barɵᵏ plant sp.
ʔɵʋx Carɵh	ʔɵʋx G'tah	ʔɵʋx Hakor	ʔɵʋx Bərcaap (2) fern sp.
ʔɵʋx Cox	ʔɵʋx Guwaaŋ	ʔɵʋx Kabaax	ʔɵʋx Biyaad plant sp.
ʔɵʋx Gapɛh	ʔɵʋx Hooŋ	ʔɵʋx K'rɛitəy	ʔɵʋx Bɵt edible mushroom sp.
ʔɵʋx Gɛmpas	ʔɵʋx Jutat	ʔɵʋx Limɵw	ʔɵʋx B'síír from *pasíír*, edible fern
ʔɵʋx Jərnɛy	ʔɵʋx Kɛlbaax (2)	ʔɵʋx Lɛɛg	ʔɵʋx Camɛɛŋ edible plant sp.
ʔɵʋx J'lax	ʔɵʋx Kɛmbuᵏ*	ʔɵʋx Malɵŋ	ʔɵʋx Cəd from *gapəd*, zingiber sp.
ʔɵʋx Kabuᵏ (2)	ʔɵʋx K'nalax (2)	ʔɵʋx Tapɛɛl	ʔɵʋx Dagax yam sp.
ʔɵʋx Kasaaw	ʔɵʋx K'nɛgwɛɛg		ʔɵʋx Gasɛᵏ palm sp.
ʔɵʋx Kasaw	ʔɵʋx Kumhaŋ		ʔɵʋx Jaay wild banana sp.
ʔɵʋx Katuᵏ (2)	ʔɵʋx Lumag		ʔɵʋx Haliᵏ plant sp.
ʔɵʋx K'ladɛw	ʔɵʋx Mataᵏ		ʔɵʋx Hɛrpix from *tapix*, zingiber sp.
ʔɵʋx Kulíd (2)	ʔɵʋx Pɛncɛd		ʔɵʋx Jarɵw pandanus sp.
ʔɵʋx Lagoh (2)	ʔɵʋx Raŋsííl		ʔɵʋx Kɛh edible plant sp.
ʔɵʋx Mahaŋ	ʔɵʋx P'rəəᵏ		ʔɵʋx K'maar palm sp.
ʔɵʋx Raaŋ	ʔɵʋx Rɛjnaaj		ʔɵʋx Kùmhaag yam sp.
ʔɵʋx R'guul	ʔɵʋx Salɵg (2)		ʔɵʋx Lapɛd from *gapɛd*, zingiber sp.
ʔɵʋx Sanol (2)	ʔɵʋx Samɵg		ʔɵʋx L'bag plant sp.

Forest Trees	Hunters' Trees	Fruit Trees	Plants
River (ʔŏŏx) – Continued			
ʔŏŏx Sowɔj	ʔŏŏx Tapoŋ		ʔŏŏx Mərkɛh — from *kɛh*, edible plant sp.
ʔŏŏx Tampaal	ʔŏŏx Tɔt		ʔŏŏx Mŏŏŋ — zingiber sp.
ʔŏŏx Tɛlor	ʔŏŏx Yahpih		ʔŏŏx Pakuᵏ — edible fern sp.
ʔŏŏx T'lambaᵏ			ʔŏŏx Sayɔj — from *sŏic*, edible fern sp.
ʔŏŏx T'ramoᵏ			ʔŏŏx Taməŋ — pandanus sp.
ʔŏŏx T'rəs*			ʔŏŏx Tapix — zingiber sp.
			ʔŏŏx ʔUud — plant sp.

T'rəs : a *j'lax* tree was lying in the river; *t'ras* means very hard.
Kɛmbʉᵏ : *kusap*, a fruit tree, is also known as *kɛmbʉᵏ*.

Waterfall (tɛŋkŏh)

Forest Trees	Hunters' Trees	Fruit Trees	Plants
Tɛŋkŏh Badŏŏx	Tɛŋkŏh Cɛrmɛer	Tɛŋkŏh Calaag	Tɛŋkŏh Baroᵏ — plant sp.
Tɛŋkŏh Bayuur	Tɛŋkŏh J'rix		Tɛŋkŏh Cadag — zingiber sp.
Tɛŋkŏh Jadaar	Tɛŋkŏh K'ʔuux		Tɛŋkŏh S'kɛᵏ — pandanus
Tɛŋkŏh Jɛx	Tɛŋkŏh Sɛntəb		Tɛŋkŏh Tapix — zingiber sp.
Tɛŋkŏh J'lax			
Tɛŋkŏh R'guul			
Tɛŋkŏh Sɛmpor			
Tɛŋkŏh Sɛŋsiŋ			

River pool (gool)

Forest Trees	Hunters' Trees	Fruit Trees	Plants
Gool Bayas	Gool C'goh	Gool Haʔoog	Gool Baroᵏ — plant sp.
Gool Bɛrbŏw	Gool Gɛnraij	Gool Jiyɛɛs	Gool Biyaad — plant sp.
Gool C'rɛŋlŏŏx	Gool Gɛntŏx	Gool K'bʉʉl*	Gool B'rawɛɛŋ — plant sp. (2)
Gool Jadɛɛr	Gool Gɛrhaar	Gool Kuriix (2)	Gool Mɛnsad — from *b'saad*, rough leaf
Gool Kabuᵏ (2)	Gool G'tah (2)	Gool Rɛhroh	Gool Pahuᵏ — plant sp.
Gool Lagoh	Gool Guwaaɲ		Gool Tamuŋ — pandanus sp.
Gool Laloᵏ	Gool ʔIpəəs (2)		
Gool Pulɛy (2)	Gool Kɛlpoŋ		
Gool Ralɛh	Gool L'ʔɛɛg		
Gool Raŋsííl (2)	Gool Rakoᵏ		
Gool R'guul (2)	Gool Sagəər		
Gool Rumpay	Gool Tagɛɛs		
Gool Tadùg	Gool Tapoŋ		
Gool Tagat			
Gool Taŋlun			
Gool Tɛŋgayoŋ			
Gool Tɛsras* (2)			
Gool T'layag			

Tɛsras : a *bɛrbŏw* tree (moluccan ironwood) fell in the river here and it remained for many years; *tɛsras*, hard.
K'bʉʉl : *sɛmpaaᵏ k'bʉʉl* is a jungle durian variety.

Island (rapag)

Forest Trees	Hunters' Trees	Fruit Trees	Plants
			Rapag Baroᵏ — plant sp.
			Rapag Lambŏᵏ — yam plants.

GROUP 1: NATURAL SPECIES II

Medical Plant	Flower	Vine	Bamboo
Swidden *(l'mog)*			
Kayaaᵏ K'mơơᵏ*	C'naap P'lad Sumbaah (2) Tanjuŋ (2)	Kɛldơŋ Manơw Papan (2)	Jɛrsɛɛp K'caaw L'hɛŋ* S'mɛɛy

K'mơơᵏ : from *k'moŋ*, a medicinal plant.
L'hɛŋ : *siyɛŋ ʔawɛn* are the bare twigs of dead bamboo.

Mountain *(jɛlmơl)*			
Cihuŋ 1596m G'rōᵏ 1196m Kasay 1676m Kayaaᵏ 1440m K'jaay* 1155m	Diyəl 1671m Hɛntəl 1526m Hɛrkơy 1834m (2) Kɛriyɛɛr 1503m Milor 1164m M'nandal 1575m R'napəd* 1928m Síríŋ 1876m S'rudɛb 1238m Suŋkùt 1624m Tahơn 1517m	C'nɛgmơg*1283m Kanjɛɛr* 1567m S'linow 1210m	Pɛnrɛɛw 1457m R'nakɛd* 1599m Sarɛŋ 1417m S'wơơr 1545m

K'jaay : the white resin of the *gooc* tree.
R'napəd : the flowers of *gapəd* zingiber plants give fragrance here.
C'nɛgmơg : many *c'mơg* vines are found here.t
Kanjɛɛr : *manjɛɛr* is a rattan species used for tying fish traps.
R'nakɛd : The bamboo hits together at the tops, making a noise, kɛd-kɛd.
S'linow : from *manơw*, rattan species.

Hill *(taŋkơl)*			
Gooc 1058m Jamuuᵏ 1053m Kasay 463m Kayaaᵏ 465m Pɛnyaaw 302m Rɛsmas 761m Taŋaar* 562m	Buŋaaᵏ 560m Hubɛɛw 600m Kaw 423m K'rɛᵏbuᵏ 607m Luŋɛɛw 1185m P'rawas 772m Sumbaah 641m	Bawəᵏ* 424m Cɛrwɛɛr* 428m Kason 671m Píŋgow 294m P'nehsɛh 414m P'nintɛs 281m Pulas* 305m R'nalơj 348m ʔUrad 1045m	Batɛᵏ 605m Bɛɛy* 853m C'nabơŋ 886m Saah 468m S'mɛɛy 307m S'wơơr 1301m

Taŋaar : a variety of *gooc* tree, the resin of which was used for making boat gum.
Bawəᵏ : also known as *kalox*, a vine chewed with betel nut.
Cɛrwɛɛr : *cɛrwíís* is a rattan species.
Pulas : many vines are twisted here; *pulas*, twisting.
Bɛɛy : *bɛɛy ʔawɛn* are the spiky new shoots of bamboo.
C'nabơŋ : *ʔawɛn gantaŋ*, giant bamboo, makes large shoots, called *c'nabơŋ*.

Medical Plant	Flower	Vine	Bamboo
Gully *(luwag)*			
Luwag Kasay 1521m Luwag Kayaaᵏ 1574m (2) Luwag K'bɔx 579m Luwag R'nadəx* 444m	Luwag K'wuy 1480m Luwag Luhɛɛw 642m Luwag Tahon 1323m Luwag Yahpɛh* 424m	Luwag G'rah 1523m	Luwag P'lakuj 499m

R'nadəx : the *s'dùx* plant is found here.
Yahpɛh : the *gapɛh* flower is found here.

Ridge *(gɛrbɔɔᵏ)*			
Gɛrbɔɔᵏ Kasay 703m Gɛrbɔɔᵏ S'dùx 1325m	Gɛrbɔɔᵏ P'rawas 441m	Gɛrbɔɔᵏ Haag 428m	Gɛrbɔɔᵏ B'sííᵏ 522m Gɛrbɔɔᵏ S'wɵɵr 1383m
Boulder *(batuᵏ)*			
		Batuᵏ G'rah	Batuᵏ B'sííᵏ
Cave *(guwɔɔᵏ)*			
	Guwɔɔᵏ Sibɛɛw		
Boulder *(batuᵏ)*			
		Batuᵏ G'rah	Batuᵏ B'sííᵏ

Sibɛɛw : the *hubɛɛw* flower is found here.

River *(ʔɵɵx)*			
ʔɵɵx Cɛlcɵɵl ʔɵɵx J'waaŋ ʔɵɵx Pɛnyaaw	ʔɵɵx Bawaŋ ʔɵɵx ʔɛndəəm ʔɵɵx Gapɛh (2) ʔɵɵx Locɛɛw ʔɵɵx Puʉn (2)	ʔɵɵx Galəər ʔɵɵx Tayug ʔɵɵx Tɛŋtɛɛx ʔɵɵx T'now	ʔɵɵx Babɵg* ʔɵɵx Gantaŋ ʔɵɵx Jɛmjɛp* ʔɵɵx Kataŋ ʔɵɵx Rantiŋ

Babɵg : *ʔawɛn pɵ̃ɵ̃g* is a species of bamboo.
Jɛmjɛp : a raft was caught in *jɛmjɛp ʔawɛn*, the fronds of bamboo, overhanging the river.

Waterfall *(tɛŋkɵh)*			
Tɛŋkɵh Manɑɑr	Tɛŋkɵh G'rɛmtɵp Tɛŋkɵh Luŋɛɛw		
River pool *(gool)*			
Gool K'bɵx		Gool Kɛnrɛn	Gool B'laaw Gool Liyaax Gool S'mɛɛy (3)
Bog *(l'baax)*			
	Payaᵏ Gambus		

GROUP 2: ANIMAL SPECIES

Tiger

Swidden (l'mog)

Cɛdʔiid	Pəŋhuluᵏ Boŋsu heard strange noises, that he suspected were made by a tiger. He climbed up a tree and then he saw six tigers below; *cɛdʔiid*, growling.
Hoʊb	A tiger made a noise, sounding like, *hoʊb, hoʊb*, at the millet field.
Kɛnhɛɛx	They had to keep watch at night because a tiger was around; *kɛɛx*, to watch out.
ʔOwiŋ	When they were cutting this swidden, they heard a tiger growling, making a sound like *ʔowiŋ*.
Rɛnʔəəh	A tiger was heard calling, making an *ʔəəl-ʔəəl* sound; *rɛnʔəəl*, bellowing.

Mountain (jɛlmoʊl)

Pɛlwaar 1439m	A tiger was caught in a spear trap, and its intestines poured out; *c'waar*, gush out.
P'rɛŋnííŋ 1539m	A man met a tiger standing on the mountain and he shouted at it but it stood still. After a few minutes the tiger jumped away; *p'rɛŋnííŋ*, not moving a muscle.

Hill (taŋkoʊl)

Balíŋ 742m (2)	A man saw a tiger sleeping and it awoke and the old man hid himself. Then the tiger returned to its sleep again and the old man escaped; *balíŋ*, tiger.
Paŋkas 578m	Dream: Taaᵏ ʔAmpís saw sambar deer bolting when the *guníg* tiger came near them; *paŋkar*, to bolt.
S'nawɛɛr 821m	This hill is the place where Raŋgɛn Lahor was attacked by a tiger. The tiger dragged his body down the hill and paced around it; *kawɛɛr*, to surround.
T'mɛnkaaᵏ 856m	They met a tiger, so they shouted a warning to the others; *tɛrkaaᵏ*, to shout a warning, *t'rɛnkaaᵏ*, a warning shout, that became *t'mɛnkaaᵏ*.

Gully (luwag)

Luwag Bɛrluh 963m	A man was up a fruit tree catching birds and the full moon cast his shadow to the ground. A tiger pounced on his shadow, thinking it was a person; *bɛrluh*, pounce.
Luwag Kapííj ʔAab 458m	A tiger made scratches on the ground; *kapííj*, scratch.
Luwag Sɛnjan 315m	Dream: a tiger pounced on its prey; *rɛmrajam*, pounce, it became *sɛnjan*.

River (ʔoʊx)

ʔOʊx Cɛŋwoʊŋ	There was a tiger attack at this river; *cɛŋwoʊŋ*, tiger attack.
ʔOʊx Kawoʊd	A tiger vomited at the river after it attacked a person; *tɛlwoʊd*, to vomit, which became *kawoʊd*.
ʔOʊx Kɛntob	A tiger caught a wild boar here and ate out the middle, so that it became two pieces; *k'toʊb*, bite in half.
ʔOʊx Kɛrpəy	They saw tiger paw prints in the sand; *k'rɛypəy*, pitted with footprints.
ʔOʊx P'lagʔag	A tiger trod on a stick and made a snap sound; *p'lag*, snap.
ʔOʊx Ratoʊh	Dream: there was a tiger attack at the river. The Taaᵏ Bɛlyan saw the tiger in his dream, and it shook the body up and down; *ratoʊh*, shake.
ʔOʊx Tandíŋ	A leopard crouched to pounce, but they shone fire torches and shouted and it left them; *tandíŋ*, bowed down.

Tree (j'huuᵏ)

Dɛriyan Kɛyhoʊy	The tiger yawned after it ate ʔAsuh Gɛndow, Pandoᵏ's little sister; *kɛyhoʊy*, yawning.

Animal

Swidden (l'mog)

ʔAyoʹy	A bear cat was caught in a *bakoʹoᵏ* trap in the tree; *ʔayay*, bear cat, which became *ʔayoʹy*.
Capɛɛr	They caught a macaque and one asked, "*Ma-loʹoᵏ capɛɛr naᵏ?*" where is that *capɛɛr*? Its real name is *capɛɛg* but it is taboo to mention the name of an animal before it is eaten.
Kayiix	They went to climb the *jiyɛɛs* tree to harvest the fruit, and a flying fox was up the tree and it flew away; *kayiix*, flying fox.
Kɛjwooj	A pangolin curled into a ball; *kɛjwooj*, curled up.

Mountain (jɛlmoʹl)

Caŋkay 1743m (2)	*Sɛgnug caŋkay*, the bull frog.
Raŋkuuᵏ 1364m	Dream: there were many langurs, chattering and making noise; *raŋkuuᵏ*, langur.
Sasoʹoᵏ Cowaᵏ 1466m	A wild dog (dhole) carcass was found here rotting, it had been killed in a fight with other dogs; *sasoʹoᵏ*, rotting, *cowaᵏ*, dog.

Hill (taŋkoʹl)

ʔAmaŋ 501m	Siamang monkeys were making loud calls; *ʔamaŋ*, siamang.
Bawaaj 615m	A storm arose because they broke a taboo while playing with a macaque monkey; *bawaaj*, macaque.
Canaŋ 849m	They trapped a wild boar; *lanaŋ*, wild boar track.
Gɛmpùd 770m	*Gɛmpùd*, large male macaque.
Gɛrgug 905m	The sound the frogs made here was like, *gug-gug-gug*.
Kajəl 1017m	Elephants left their big foot prints in the mud; *bəkajəl*, stamping.
K'nirab 484m	A man caught a *kɛnrab* fish and he kept it to himself and after a day he died. In Temiar tradition, this fish is a *gɛnhaaᵏ* food, that must be shared, otherwise, it can cause death.
Lamboʹy 364m	*Lamboʹy* (or *biday*) is the name of a mythical creature that was created when a mat blew into the river and transmogrified.
L'jəx 451m	*L'jəx*, a flying squirrel.
Paŋkas 604m	Dream: sambar deer bolted; *paŋkar*, to bolt.
Raŋkɛŋ 392m	Here they found an animal carcass; *raŋkɛŋ*, skeleton.
Tɛrtɛɛr 797m	A lizard ran off, making a noise with its tail like, *tɛɛr-tɛɛr*.

Gully (luwag)

Luwag Barɛɛw 1553m	A rotting tapir was found here a long time ago; *barɛɛw*, tapir.
Luwag Bawaaj 587m	*Bawaaj*, pig-tailed macaque.
Luwag Gɛmpùd 767m	A lone male pig-tailed macaque was encountered here; *gɛmpùd*.
Luwag J'rɛnʔiin 646m	The siamang monkeys were making a sound like *ʔiin, ʔiin*.
Luwag Tampax 480m	*Cɛp ʔāmpax*, a flying squirrel.

Boulder (batuᵏ)

Batuᵏ Rɛnʔuy	*Haʔuy* or *ʔaŋkuuy*, is an edible frog with poisonous skin.

Animal	
Cave *(guwɔɔ^{k})*	
Guwɔɔ^{k} K′lɛrcɛɛr	When the bats fly out in large numbers they make a flapping noise, *k′lɛrcɛɛr.*
Guwɔɔ^{k} Lawaar	*Cɛp lawaar,* is a term used for bats, which nest in the cave.
River *(ˀơơx)*	
ˀƠơx ˀAmpax	*Cɛp ˀāmpax*, a flying squirrel.
ˀƠơx ˀAncōh	*ˀAncōh,* a flying squirrel with a short tail.
ˀƠơx B′rɛdlɛɛd	*K′díig b′rɛdlɛɛd* is a squirrel with a stripy tail.
ˀƠơx B′rɛdlɛɛd	A striped snake was seen; *b′rɛdlɛɛd,* striped.
ˀƠơx Cawơơ^{k}	A monkey's head fell into the river, as a leopard ate it in the tree; *cawơơ^{k}*, head.
ˀƠơx J′rɛskaas	A porcupine raised its spines; *j′rɛskaas,* porcupine.
ˀƠơx Kajít	*Sɛgnug kajɛ̄ɛ̄^{k}* is a tortoise.
ˀƠơx Kambíŋ	A tiger attacked a goat, and dragged it to the river; *kambíŋ*, goat.
ˀƠơx Kapur (2)	*K′bəə^{k} kapur* are water snails. The shells are used as lime, to chew with betel nut.
ˀƠơx Karaaj	*Sɛgnug karaaj* is a mud-dwelling tortoise.
ˀƠơx K′sơơ^{k}	There was some rotting fish at the river; *sơơ^{k}*, to rot.
ˀƠơx Kudoŋ	*Taju^{k} r′laay kudơŋ* is a species of python.
ˀƠơx Lasaar	*Cɛp lasaar*, giant bats.
ˀƠơx L′jùx	*Cɛp l′jùx,* a species of flying squirrel.
ˀƠơx Piya^{k}	*Kaa^{k} piya^{k}* is a species of fish.
ˀƠơx P′nincơơŋ	Water snails were chopped to extract the meat; *p′níncơơŋ,* chopping.
ˀƠơx R′laay	*Taju^{k} r′laay* is the python.
ˀƠơx Sirah	Langurs cackled in the morning; *sɛrkah,* to cackle.
ˀƠơx Sisí^{k}	After cleaning fish at the river fish scales covered the sand; *sisí^{k}*, scales.
ˀƠơx Sumyaŋ	Kaa^{k} sumyaŋ, a catfish.
ˀƠơx Tampɛl	*Tampɛl,* the slow loris.
ˀƠơx Waaj	Bullfrogs at the river borrow in the sand with their claws; *k′waaj,* to scrape.
Waterfall *(tɛŋkơh)*	
Tɛŋkơh Babooŋ	*Bɛŋbooŋ* are tadpoles.
Tɛŋkơh Hɛrwooj	Dream: there was a pangolin in the dream, at this waterfall; *wɛjwooj*, pangolin.
Tɛŋkơh Kasiŋ	A deer fell down the waterfall as a tiger chased it; *kasíŋ*, sambar deer.
Tɛŋkơh Kawíib	A bear fell in the river and rotted; *kawíib*, bear.
Tɛŋkơh Tayaas	An otter chewed through a fish trap and ate all the fisht; *tuyaas*, to chew through.
River pool *(gool)*	
Gool Buhyaa^{k}	*Buhyaa^{k}*, crocodiles, were believed to inhabit this pool.
Gool Hagaab	A rhinoceros fell into the river pool and died there and rotted; *hagaab*, rhinoceros.
Gool Lubơŋ	This pool was known to have a python; *lubơŋ*, hole.
Gool Sˀˀɛɛb	*Sˀˀɛɛb* is another name for *sɛgnug pɛlˀɛd,* a river turtle.
Gool Tajuu^{k}	A snake rotted in the river; *tajuu^{k}*, snake.
Gool Tɛnyu^{k}	A bear cat fell in the river and died; *tɛnyu^{k}*, bearcat.
Gool Timbəl	A snake suddenly swam by; *timbəl*, to appear.

Bird	
Swidden *(l'mog)*	
ʔɛxʔaax	Crows nested here and made much noise; *ʔɛgʔaag*, crow.
Jasaar	Dream: giant bats were in the trees; *cɛp lasaar*, bats, which became *jasaar*.
Jɛrhoˀh	Named after the *cɛp hɛhhoˀh*, the short-tailed green magpie.
Kaləŋ	The call of the rhinoceros hornbill is heard here, sounding like *k'ləŋ*.
K'liboo^k	*Cɛp k'liboo^k* is an owl species that was seen nesting here in a tree trunk.
Pɛrloŋ	*Cɛp s'mɛrloŋ*, white-winged black jay, makes a call like *s'ruloŋ*. It is taboo to mimic the call of the bird and hence the place was named differently.
Rɛnloŋ	Also named after the *cɛp s'mɛrloŋ* bird.
Mountain *(jɛlmoˀl)*	
Bawoˀl 1599m	*Bawoˀl*, another name for *cɛp t'wal*, the yellow-throated barbet.
Hill *(taŋkoˀl)*	
K'liboo^k 333m	*Cɛp k'liboo^k* is an owl species.
P'nawɛɛy 1082m	*Cɛp t'ranɛ^k*, the chequer-throated woodpecker. When it is heard calling "*wɛɛy, wɛɛy*." it is a sign that the tiger is about.
Taʔəəj 283m	*Cɛp taʔəəj*, pouched hornbill.
Gully *(luwag)*	
Luwag Baroˀw 424m	*Cɛp baroˀw*, the straw-headed bulbul, is often seen at the Lɛmpaar River.
Ridge *(gɛrbɔɔ^k)*	
Gɛrbɔɔ^k Caŋwoˀoj 868m	*Caŋwoˀoj*, the brown wood-owl.
Gɛrbɔɔ^k H$\overline{ɛ\overline{ɛ}}^k$ 879m	*Cɛp tɛrhɛɛr*, the dark hawk-cuckoo, its call sounds like, *h$\overline{ɛ\overline{ɛ}}^k$*.
Gɛrbɔɔ^k Raw 419m	A bird's call was often heard here, like *raw, raw*.
Gɛrbɔɔ^k Tibaw 393m (2)	*Cɛp toˀgtɛbaw*, the nightjar.
Cave *(guwɔɔ^k)*	
Guwɔɔ^k Layaŋ	*Cɛp layaŋ* are swallows, which nest at this cave.
River *(ʔoˀox)*	
ʔOˀox Balyɛx	*Cɛp balyɛx*, the bushy-crested hornbill.
ʔOˀox D'kug	*Cɛp d'kug*, the white-crested hornbill.
ʔOˀox G'ləəŋ	Hornbills were calling out, like *g'ləəŋ, g'ləəŋ*.
ʔOˀox Liyoŋ	*Cɛp ciyuŋ* , the hill minor bird.
ʔOˀox S'mɛrloŋ	*Cɛp s'mɛrloŋ*, the white-winged black jay.
Island *(rapag)*	
Rapag Layaŋ	Swallows fly over the water, dipping; *rapag*, island, *layaŋ*, barn swallow.
Tree *(j'huu^k)*	
J'lax Jɛrhoh	A bird call was heard at the *j'lax* tree, like *hoh, hoh*.

Insect	
Swidden (l'mog)	
Jaŋwaar	*Jaŋwaar*, a species of small black bee.
Kaləəh	They found scorpions here; Malay, *kalajenking*, scorpion.
Sɛrmaar	*Sɛrmaar* are ant tunnels made of earth
Tagʊʊɲ	*Tagʊʊɲ* are large black ants.
Mountain (jɛlmoˈl)	
Capʊg 1457m	*Capʊg*, a kind of millipede.
Hill (taŋkoˈl)	
Jaŋwaar 558m	*Jaŋwaar*, a species of small black bee.
R'jaaw 444m	*S'muj r'jaaw*, a species of wasp that nests in a hole of a tree.
Gully (lʉwag)	
Luwag Kərpəg 551m	*Kɛrpəx*, a species of tree-dwelling beetle.
Luwag L'maay 388m	*K'maay*, grubs, which became *l'maay*.
Ridge (gɛrbɔɔᵏ)	
Gɛrbɔɔᵏ Kancʊʊŋ 549m	*Kancʊʊŋ*, a preying mantis.
River (ʔʊʊx)	
ʔʊʊx Cadoŋ	Red ants were here, which point their rear ends upward; *candoŋ*, to stick up.
ʔʊʊx Kajex	*Kabɛd kajex*, fire ants, that come out at night and have a painful bite.
ʔʊʊx Kʼʔɛɛb	*Kʼʔɛɛb*, centipede.
ʔʊʊx K'lɛdbad	*K'maay k'lɛdbad*, a swarm of millipedes, entered their shelter.
ʔʊʊx K'rɛlbool	*K'rɛlbool*, is the pill millipede.
ʔʊʊx Laɲíír (2)	*S'muj laɲíír*, a species of wasp.
ʔʊʊx Sɛrmaar	*Kabɛd sɛrmaar* is an ant species that was found here.
ʔʊʊx Tagʊʊɲ	*Kabɛd tagʊʊɲ*, black ants with a sore bite.
ʔʊʊx Takʊy	*Takʊy*, a species of lizard.
ʔʊʊx Tanoŋ	*Tanoŋ*, dragonfly.
Cliff (ʔamparr)	
ʔAmparr ʔɛij	*K'maay ʔɛij* is a name for the millipede.

GROUP 3: ENVIRONMENTAL

Environment	
Swidden *(l'mog)*	
ʔɛndiŋ	The land rises up steeply; *tandiŋ*, rising up.
B'lukar	The old swidden here has overgrown with brush; Malay, *b'lukar*, brush land.
J'rɛntaaŋ	The sun shone through the tree canopy; *j'rɛntaaŋ*, holes.
Pantɛy	The river is full of sand; *pantɛy*, sand.
Paax	The place is located on the side of the hill; *paax*, above.
R'lơơy	The home was built across the river; *lơơy*, to wade across.
R'sɛɛm	It rained on them during the planting; *r'sɛɛm*, fine rain.
Sapɛd	Dream: the leaves rustled in the wind, and he said, "*Sapɛd l'lapɛd*".
Sɛrbəər	An abundance of ferns covered the place; *bəər*, ferns.
Tandíŋ	A tree was cut down and its base went up in the air; *tandiŋ*, bowing.
Mountain *(jɛlmoʻl)*	
Bərlɛɛy 1668m	The mountain top is bright; *bərlɛɛh*, clear.
B'rɛlhɛ̄ɛ̄l 1680m	The rocks are pitted with holes; *b'rɛlhɛ̄ɛ̄l*, pitted.
G'mərpɛd 1277m	The wind blows on this hill; *g'mərpɛd*, leaves rustling.
J'rɛŋkaŋ 1961m	The trees here look like bones; *j'rɛŋkaŋ*, skeletons.
Kasuh 1031m	The ground here is soft due to pine needles; *kasuh*, soft ground.
Kəd 1318m	The mountain has the shape of a pregnant woman; *kəd*, womb
Lɛmyəb 1653m	It was evening when they reached this mountain top; *lɛbyəb*, growing dark.
Lɛntííŋ 1299m	The ridge is straight; *p'rɛndííŋ*, straight.
Nawɛh 1489m	Dream: a dead branch was about to fall; *na-ʔawih*, wobbling.
Nyɛbyaab 1426m	Dream: the sun was setting; *na-nyaab* or *nyɛbnyaab*, a red sky.
Pɛrsuud 1587m	Dream: the ground was uncomfortable, due to many tree roots; *p'rasuud*, lumpy.
Pɛɛl 1337m	A swidden was planted but nothing much grew; *pɛɛl*, bald.
Saŋgíd 1305m	Two trees were rubbing together; *ʔaŋgíd*, rubbing.
Sɛmrajɛm 1660m	The mountain is full of flowers blowing about; *sɛmrajɛm*, swaying.
S'nantííŋ 1317m	The hill is straight; *s'nantííŋ*, straight.
Sơʻid 1850m	If one stands at the Bərtax River one can see the whole shape of the mountain, from the bottom right to its three peaks; *sơʻoj*, complete.
S'raŋɛm 1315m	Dream: it was getting dark on the mountain; *b'rɛm-rɛm*, dark of sky.
S'rɛmjap 1429m	The wind blows on this hill top; *s'rɛmjap*, cold.
Hill *(taŋkoʻl)*	
B'kah 1118m	A rock was split in the middle; *b'kah*, broken.
B'rơg 369m	They found water on this hill; *bar-ʔơơx*, having water.
C'raŋ 480m	The hill top was very bright; Malay, *terang*, bright.
C'rɛɛm 914m (2)	The ground is full of sharp rocks; *c'rɛɛm*, broken rocks.
C'rɛɛm 648m	The place here was clear with no trees; *c'rɛɛs*, clear.
Kubax 702m	This place is a mud hole; *kubax*, always muddy.
Lɛŋdaaŋ 1115m	The ridge curves round; *halɛŋdaaŋ*, curved.

Environment	
Hill *(taŋkoʼl)* – *Continued*	
Nolnɛɛl 644m	There was a rock that wobbled; *dulnɛɛl*, to wobble
Sɛnduŋ 643m	The river is boggy; *sɛnduŋ*, bog.
Sidaij 1149m	The sun was shining in the afternoon; *sidaij*, bright sun.
Tʼhʊʊr 766m	It is windy on this hill-top; *tʼhʊʊr*, windy.
Tʼruluj 892m	The hillside is steep; *tʼruluj*, steep.
Gully *(luwag)*	
Luwag Jʼnʊʊd 193m	There is a natural water spring near here; *jʼnʊʊd*, spring.
Luwag Kʼrap 826m	The ground is sunken; *karap*, sunken.
Luwag Pɛrhɛɛr 293m	The gully is narrow; *pɛrhɛɛr*, narrow.
Ridge *(gɛrbɔɔᵏ)*	
Gɛrbɔɔᵏ Batuᵏ 186m	There is a large rock on this ridge; *batuᵏ*, rock.
Gɛrbɔɔᵏ Gɛjtʊj 675m	The hill is truncated, cut off before it reaches the river; *gɛjtʊj*, broken.
Gɛrbɔɔᵏ Líŋkʊŋ 307m	The ridge bends round; *lɛŋkoᵏ*, bent.
Gɛrbɔɔᵏ Pʼrɛdhiid 1744m	The wind blows on this ridge *pʼrɛdhiid*, cool breeze.

The author, standing at the hanging rock, at the Jɛŋhuŋ River, in 2013. (Credit: ʔAríf Pandaᵏ)

Environment

Boulder (batuᵏ)

Batuᵏ ʔAsaad	This giant, 50-foot high rock is shaped like a pumpkin; ʔasaad, pumpkin.
Batuᵏ Cɛrpoɔ̆r	The rock here points downward toward the ground; cɛrpoɔ̆r, pointing downward.
Batuᵏ J'rɛntííl	This rock hangs over the river; j'rɛntiil, hanging.
Batuᵏ K'ramad	A rock that is believed to be put here at the beginning; k'ramad, ancient.

Cave (guwɔɔᵏ)

Guwɔɔᵏ Layɛg	The cave is very dark inside; layɛg, night.

River (ʔoɔ̆x)

ʔoɔ̆x ʔAŋəl	This river is very short; taŋəl, short.
ʔoɔ̆x Bərtax	The Bərtax river is often reddish; bartɛx, earthy, which became, bərtax.
ʔoɔ̆x Bijɛh	Traces of tin can be found here in the sand; bijɛh, tin.
ʔoɔ̆x B'laʔər	The pool at the river mouth was once deep and green in colour; b'laʔər, green.
ʔoɔ̆x B'rɛnhooŋ	The river here disappears into holes; b'rɛnhooŋ, holes.
ʔoɔ̆x Cɛghaag	There is a pounding sound of a waterfall; c'rɛghaag, pounding.
ʔoɔ̆x Cɛŋlùx	The river water is reddish in colour; cɛŋlùx, reddish.
ʔoɔ̆x C'nuntùg	A tree was stuck between a j'lax tree and a luwaaᵏ creeper; cuntùg, stuck between.
ʔoɔ̆x C'rɛghaag	The water splashes on the rocks; c'rɛghaag, splashing.
ʔoɔ̆x Cumrah	The rocks at the river mouth are sharp; batuᵏ b'cùmrah, sharp rocks.
ʔoɔ̆x G'rɛm	Batuᵏ gɛŋrɛm is a black rock found here, like shale.
ʔoɔ̆x Jɛŋrɛŋ	A man was angry one day; b'jɛŋrɛŋ, red-faced.
ʔoɔ̆x J'noɔ̆d	There is a natural spring near here; j'noɔ̆d, spring.
ʔoɔ̆x Kɛnsɛɛy	The river is so small it drips off a rock; bɛyb'rɛɛy, trickling.
ʔoɔ̆x K'tɛɛd	A man put his foot in between two rocks and it was stuck; k'tɛɛb, stuck.
ʔoɔ̆x Lɛrbor	Green algae grows in the mud here; lɛrbor, algae.
ʔoɔ̆x Paaŋ	The river bank collapsed during a flood, and it became like a dam; paaŋ, dam.
ʔoɔ̆x P'rɛlcoɔ̆l	The rocks glint in the river here; p'rɛlcoɔ̆l, glinting.
ʔoɔ̆x Rapag	The river has an island; rapag, island.
ʔoɔ̆x Rɛɛx	The river bank collapsed; rɛɛx, collapse.
ʔoɔ̆x Santəj	A bɛrboͦw or ironwood tree lay in the river for many years; təj, wood rot.
ʔoɔ̆x Taboͦh	A tree at the river has a large hole in it; taboͦh, a hole in a tree.
ʔoɔ̆x Wɛgwoɔ̆g	They saw a rainbow; na-woɔ̆g, it arose, wɛgwoɔ̆g, arising, the tterm for a rainbow.

Waterfall (tɛŋkoͦh)

Tɛŋkoͦh Cabaax	The water splits up like branches; cabaax, branch.
Tɛŋkoͦh Cagool	The waterfall has isolated rock pools; cagool, pool.
Tɛŋkoͦh C'rɛdhiid	The wind blew and it was cool; p'rɛdhiid, cool.
Tɛŋkoͦh ʔIlõŋᵏ	The waterfall has rock pools; b'kɛnlõᵏ, having holes, hence ʔilõᵏ.
Tɛŋkoͦh Kancaaŋ	The waterfall makes a spray and a rainbow can often be seen; k'lɛncaaŋ, splashing.
Tɛŋkoͦh Lɛlʔííl	The water here makes waves; lɛlʔííl, making waves.
Tɛŋkoͦh Mũũᵏ	Fish can't swim up this waterfall; mũũᵏ, fish barrier.

Environment	
Waterfall *(tɛŋkoʰ)* – *Continued*	
Tɛŋkoʰ Pancur	There is a channel in the rock, like a gutter; *pancur*, gutter.
Tɛŋkoʰ Pɛwp'lūūw	Water plunges into the pool, *p'lūūw, p'lūūw; pɛwp'lūūw*, plunging.
Tɛŋkoʰ Pooj	The waterfall cascades, sounding like *pooj-pooj*.
Tɛŋkoʰ Rapag	There is an island at the waterfall; *rapag*, island.
Tɛŋkoʰ Rɛwrow	The water falls here making the noise, *row-row*, hence, *rɛwrow*.
Tɛŋkoʰ Saŋíd	The waterfall makes a gusting sound; *saŋíd*, gusting.
Tɛŋkoʰ S'nankaad	The waterfall throws water; *sankaad*, to splash
Tɛŋkoʰ S'rɛɲwííɲ	The river makes channels; *s'rɛɲwííɲ*, channeling.
River pool *(gool)*	
Gool B'laŋaaᵏ	The pool is round, like a cooking pot or wok; *b'laŋaaᵏ*, wok.
Gool K'lɛŋwííɲ	There are whirlpools; *lɛŋwííɲ*, whirling.
Gool Nyoʰg	The river pool is like a hole; *nyoʰg*, hole.
Gool Rapag	There is an island; *rapag*, island.
Gool Sɛws'row	The water makes a noise like *s'row*.
Gool S'rɛnyɛb	There is a gorge; *s'rɛnyɛb*, rock walls.
Inland pool *(cagool)*	
Cagol Tímbul	The water in this pool rises and falls without a river filling it; *tímbul*, rising.
Bog *(l'baax)*	
L'baax Sɛnduŋ	The source of the Puyan River; *sɛnduŋ*, bog, *l'baax*, mud.
Payak Məndaŋ	The land collapsed here and it looked like a wall; *məndaŋ*, mud wall.
Spring *(j'nooʰd)*	
J'nooʰd Gugag	The path is narrow, so that many animals fall into the water; *dugag*, narrow.
Tree *(j'huuᵏ)*	
Dɛriyan S'dɛl	Dream: a dream of the long valley; *s'dɛl*, long.

Weather	
Swidden *(l'mog)*	
Gərgɛg	The sky darkened and a storm came up; *gərgɛb*, a dark sky.
Lapoʰg	They couldn't burn the swidden because it rained too much; *lapoʰj*, sodden.

Weather

Mountain (jɛlmoʹl)

Bɛlhiiw 1429m	Dream: the wind blew; *b'giiw*, the name of the wind (taboo).
ꞋƐŋkuuᵏ 1808m	There was loud thunder; *ʔɛŋkuuᵏ*, thunder.
Lɛmŋoʹom 1769m	The sky was gloomy, about to rain; *rɛmŋoʹom*, gloomy.
Nyərnyɛb 1076m	The sky darkened suddenly, about to rain; *nyərnyɛb*, sudden dark sky.
S'naŋkad 1611m	It was raining and windy and they said, "*Hoj na-s'naŋkad*", it's gusty.
S'nurow 1595m	They heard the sound of rain coming; *s'nurow*, the sound of rain.

Hill (taŋkoʹl)

P'gas 1190m	Dream: the wind was blowing strongly; *p'ragaas*, noise of gusting wind.
P'risoʹoy 325m	It was windy; *p'risoʹoy*, wind before the rain.
Rɛmŋoʹom 954m	The sky darkened; *rɛmŋoʹom*, a gloomy sky.
S'rikɔɔb 266m	The sky was dark with rain clouds; *s'rikɔɔb*, darkening.

Ridge (gɛrbɔɔᵏ)

Tɛᵏ S'nurow 1368m	Dream: Taaᵏ K'lusar heard rain; *s'nurow*, sound of rain.

Boulder (batuᵏ)

Batuᵏ C'gur	Dream: he heard the sound of rain, *c'gur*.

River (ʔoʹox)

ꞋOʹox Gɔɔb	The sky became gloomy, as if a storm was coming; *sɛrkɔɔb*, gloomy sky.
ꞋOʹox Pataag	The rain fell on the roofing and made a loud spattering sound; *sɛgpataag*, dripping.

Waterfall (tɛŋkoʹh)

Tɛŋkoʹh ꞋƐŋkuuᵏ	Dream: it thundered at the waterfall; *ʔɛŋkuuᵏ*, thunder.

A survey team stands in front of ꞋƐnkuuᵏ waterfall.

GROUP 4: HUMAN FACTORS

Event	
Swidden *(l'mog)*	
Batɛŋ	Ants swarmed inside the cooking bamboo and when one of them threw it away hastily; *bajɛŋ*, to toss away, which became *batɛŋ*.
ʔɛntɛɛb	They were digging up a rat's burrow, and one of them got his hand stuck in the hole; *k'tɛɛb*, stuck, which became *ʔɛntɛɛb*.
Habog	A Semai soldier, ʔAnjaŋ Platun, who worked at the post in 1980, buried a charm in a packet of ash here, in order to kill people with its power; *habog*, ash.
Kəmboŋ	They played in the river, filling up their sarongs with air and floating on the water; *kəmboŋ*, to bloat.
Puŋgəŋ	They were fetching water in bamboo flasks and the water made a *gooŋ* sound as it sloshed, which became *gəŋ*, or *puŋgəŋ*.
Sajaaᵏ	One old man claimed that he saw a tiger but they thought he was just making up a story; *sajaaᵏ*, making it up.
Sigaŋ	During the aerial attack on the swiddens, in 1954, the attacking aeroplane used its machine-guns on the homes below; *síŋgan*, machine-gun, which became *sigaŋ*.
S'rijoʻh	They were digging up yams and the young ones were running about, and they said, "*ʔAgoᵏ ham-joʻh!*" don't disturb the work!
Mountain *(jɛlmoʻl)*	
ʔAyaap 912m	Long ago, an old woman and her house were transported onto this mountain by magic and when she saw where she had landed she cried. Seeing that, her dog told her not to cry; *ʔayaap*, don't cry.
Capaaᵏ 1585m	They said, "Don't waste time we need to go." From *cintaaᵏ*, to delay.
C'pəəs 1554m	A man was searching for something in his basket and he disturbed his companion; *c'pəəs*, to disturb someone in their sleep.
Rɛnipəər 1618m	It became dark and they couldn't see the path and they fumbled along; *rɛhpəər*, fumbling along, *rɛnipəər*, a fumbling.
Rɛnupoʻw 1605m	The bamboo popped in the fire, making a sound *poʻw*; *rɛmupoʻw*, popping of bamboo in a fire.
Sɛglapoʻog 1258m	The cloth came undone and all their belongings fell on the ground; *sɛglapoʻog*, to drop all over the place.
Sɛmlayaam 1249m	They stuffed so many flowers and fragrant leaves in their baskets that they bounced about; *sɛmlayaam*, bouncing about.
S'nuŋùd 1661m	A woman was crying, and her husband asked her, "*Ha-suŋùd?*" are you hungry?
Hill *(taŋkoʻl)*	
Bayoʻl 691m	The rain was coming, and they hurried to build shelters to keep dry; *ʔɛlʔoʻl*, to hurry up, which became *bayoʻl*.
Taŋkoʻl Cɛnlaar	A child died here in the house and they covered the house over with palm leaves and left it; *cɛnlaar*, a covering.
Gɛjgíijwɛɛd 938m	Taaᵏ ʔAmpís was warming himself by the fire and he sat too close and his loin cloth caught fire; *gɛjgíij*, burning, *wɛɛd*, privates.
Hɛmpaal 479m	They beat the *d'koʻh* fruits here to obtain the stones; *paan*, beat with a rod.
J'lantíís 510m	They said, "*Ja bʔadíís*", don't walk about, because they shouldn't walk near the *jiyɛɛs* trees before the harvest, or the fruits will be spoiled; which became, *j'lantíís*.

Event

Hill *(taŋkoʼl)* – Continued

J'nulaŋ 783m	Two men had a contest, and pulled on each end of a stick; *j'nulaŋ*, contest.
Julaaᵏ 686m	A man met a bear and had to keep himself unseen; *julaaᵏ*, secret.
Ɖulŋaal 1147m	Two men went bird-gumming in the early morning,while still dark. One of them made a sign to the other when he had found the tree, waving a burning bamboo torch; *ŋaal*, wave, *ŋulŋaal*, waving.
P'ralaaw 711m	A tataaᵏ halaaᵏ showed off by jumping from one rock to another, but he fell and died, and he himself became a rock; *p'laaw*, to fly using magic power.
Rɛwroʼow 806m	Here they were pulling down rattan from the trees; *roʼow*, pull down.
Sɛmbul 605m	In order to flee from danger during the fighting, they wrapped up their small children to carry them; *s'bul*, to wrap, *sɛmbul*, wrapping.
Tumpoh 567m	A group of people known among the locals as *tumpoh* planted a flag on this hill; from English, topo, topography mappers.

Gully *(luwag)*

Luwag Lambar 219m	During the period of fighting between government and Communists, they signaled to the others to flee for safety; *lambar*, signal.
Luwag Pɛnˀəh 785m	The old man said, "ˀAgoᵏ pɛhˀəh", don't go out anywhere, because there was danger of meeting a wild animal.
Luwag Tɛndəp 1457m	They watched langurs in the bamboo where they were sleeping, so that they could blowpipe them in the morning; *tɛndəp*, watching to prevent escape.

Ridge *(gɛrbɔɔᵏ)*

Gɛrbɔɔᵏ Biyɛᵏ 761m	A Jehai man said, "Bi-yɛᵏ", give me some, as he wanted to eat some manioc.
Gɛrbɔɔᵏ B'kooh 630m	They were digging roots and got covered with mud; *b'kooh*, brown or muddy.
Gɛrbɔɔᵏ Kandaŋ 581m	They built bamboo walls to enclose a herd of wild boars; *kandaŋ*, animal pen.
Gɛrbɔɔᵏ Tayããŋ 569m	A man was bitten by a tick from a boar's nest and he had to pull it off; *cayaaŋ*, spread wide the legs.

Boulder *(batuᵏ)*

Batuᵏ D'raŋoʼg	A group saw tiger eyes shining in the dark. They waited at this rock until the morning, stuck there because of the tiger; *dɛgdəŋoʼg*, wishing to go home, which became, *d'raŋoʼg*.
Batuᵏ Jaŋkaar	Two Menriq brothers were hunting, and it was raining. The older brother was feeling ill and told the younger to make a fire, and so he gathered sticks, but the fire stone and cotton were all wet so he couldn't make a fire. The older brother died at the place because of the cold; *jaŋkaar*, sticks.
Batuᵏ Sɛŋsoʼŋ	Three men were hunting and they slept up on this rock. During their sleep, Taaᵏ Rawɛy snored and made a sound like *sɛŋsoʼŋ-sɛŋsoʼŋ*.

Cave *(guwɔɔᵏ)*

Guwɔɔᵏ G'rɛndoʼŋ	While fishing here, one of them carried fish in a bamboo tube, tucked into his loin cloth. But the bamboo slipped out and fell on the rock below, making a sound, *g'r'doʼŋ*, so they called the cave they ate in, *g'rɛndoʼŋ*.
Guwɔɔᵏ L'nayuur	They went bat hunting and warmed their bamboo sticks in the fire so they could light them easily to shine for bats; *layuur*, to warm over a fire, *l'nayur*, warming.
Guwɔɔᵏ Rɛnipuy	They hunted bats by hitting them with sticks; *r'pəh*, swipe, but accidentally, ˀAlaŋ Rantaw said "R'puy", hence the name became *rɛnipuy*.

Event	
River (ʔoˑóx)	
ʔOˑóx Bagəd	They saw something here which was amazing; *bagəd*, amazed.
ʔOˑóx Baraŋ	They dropped all their belongings into the river; *baraŋ*, things.
ʔOˑóx Cɛŋgɛg	The monkeys were escaping hunters and one of them fell to the ground and was caught and strangled; *c'gɛg*, to strangle, *cɛŋgɛg*, strangling.
ʔOˑóx C'nahɔɔd	A man promised to go with a friend but then didn't go; *p'rɛnhɔɔd*, to promise in vain.
ʔOˑóx C'naróy	A man went rat trapping, using *soˑic* nuts as bait; *ʔɛ-c'róy k'dííg*, to leave bait for rats, *c'naróy*, baiting.
ʔOˑóx Jɛŋhuŋ	A bamboo tube fell onto a rock in the river, making a gong sound, *g'rahooŋ*.
ʔOˑóx K'nɛdwɔɔd	Here they climbed up the rock; *cawɔɔd* or *kɛdwɔɔd*, to climb up, became *k'nɛdwɔɔd*.
ʔOˑóx K'ralul	The men sat here to rest, and the loin cloth of one of them came loose, showing his balls; *k'ralul*, stones.
ʔOˑóx Ləəŋ	A *ləg*, blow-dart quiver, was dropped in the river and the cotton came out.
ʔOˑóx Lɛrləər	The children climbed up the rock and reached out hands for help, as the rock was slippery; *ləər*, to reach out, *lɛrləər*, reaching.
ʔOˑóx Palɛɛs	*Palɛɛs-paloˑs* means going there and coming back here again (going all over the place).
ʔOˑóx Pɛlcəl	They prodded the sand in the river looking for turtles; *cəl*, to prod the ground.
ʔOˑóx Píncoˑóŋ	One day they were chopping snail shells, putting the edible meat into bamboo, and the shells in a leaf to make kapur lime; *cɛncoˑóŋ*, chopping, which became *Píncoˑóŋ*.
ʔOˑóx S'raŋɛᵏ	Quartz stones are found at this river, used for making sparks to light a fire. One time they couldn't make sparks; *səŋɛᵏ*, quiet, *s'raŋɛᵏ*, no sparks.
ʔOˑóx T'rɛy	Thy dropped fruits on the ground and they rolled down the slope; *kɛrlɛy*, rolling.
ʔOˑóx Wəəx	A man's shadow was cast on the water; *woˑóg*, shadow, which became *wəəx*.
Tree (j'huuᵏ)	
Sɛmpaaᵏ Hɛbhɔɔb	There were so many fruits at the *sɛmpaaᵏ k'ladas* tree, a jungle durian, that they were excited; *hɛmhɔɔp*, to get excited.

Feeling	
Mountain (jɛlmoˑl)	
Hũũlhĩl 1491m	It feels as if the mountain moves, because the wind blows so strongly. *hũũl*, to blow.
Jahid 1372m	Dream: Taaᵏ K'lusar dreamed of this place and it was cold there; *j'həd*, biting cold.
Lɛrʔor 1588m	Dream: it was the dry season and hot; *lɛrʔor*, hot, sweating.
P'rɛdhiid 1205m	Dream: a breeze blew up there at night; *p'rɛdhiid*, cool.
S'mɛriyəh 1675m	This place has so many flowers, so they say, "*S'mɛriyəh*", how beautiful.
Hill (taŋkoˑl)	
Tərbɛh 486m	It was very hot; *sərwɛh*, to make uncomfortable, which became *tərbɛh*.
Gully (luwag)	
Luwag Bataŋ Yəᵏ 643m	This is a mountains pass on the path to B'riix. When this gully is crossed it means that the place one came from is left behind; *bataŋ*, hill, *yəᵏ*, behind.

Feeling	
Ridge (*gɛrbɔɔᵏ*)	
Gɛrbɔɔᵏ B′gɔŋ 956m	This ridge is long, and walking up it makes one feel thirsty; *pɛŋp′gɔŋ*, thirsty.
Boulder (*batuᵏ*)	
Batuᵏ ʔAsal Rɛnapəm	Dream: it felt very cold; *rɛnapəm*, biting cold.
River (*ʔoʊx*)	
ʔOʊx Cɛnroᵏ	They had nothing to cook or eat; *cɛnroᵏ*, hunger,
ʔOʊx Sɛnmah	They were very hungry and weak; *lɛhmah*, weak.

Person	
Swidden (*l′mog*)	
ʔAhíŋ	ʔAhíŋ Bərlɛy was born here.
Cakob	An old woman, Jaaᵏ Cakob, crawled inside a mahogany tree here and died.
Pundoŋ	Tataaᵏ Pundoŋ capsized his raft and his bush knife fell in the river. It got stuck in the rocks and then transmogrified into a rock itself.
Síntam	Sintam ʔAnjaŋ, son of ʔAnjaŋ Tɛŋah, was born here.
Mountain (*jɛlmoʊl*)	
ʔƏnɛŋrɛy 1685m	Dream: The call of the *cɛp toʊgroʊh*, the yellow-throated barbet, was calling and it reminded the old man of a woman, named ʔƏnɛŋrɛy.
Səmnaᵏ 1459m	A woman was born here, Səmnaᵏ, on the path to the S′ŋaaᵏ river in Perak, and she was named after that river.
Yaŋʔoʊl / ʔAboʊŋ 1032m	Dream: a person was here, whose name was Jaŋʔoʊl. A more recent name is ʔAboʊŋ, the name of a Temiar woman.
Hill (*taŋkoʊl*)	
D′ríís 450m	D′ríís is the name of a Temiar man who was born here.
Hantar 1147m	Hantar K′lusar, the elder brother of Pəŋhuluᵏ P′diᵏ, was born here.
R′nayol 795m	The name of a Menriq woman from long ago.
Gully (*luwag*)	
Luwag Bajɛg 1196m	A man from Jadɛɛr was seen here, Taaᵏ Bajɛg.
Luwag Juwalɛy 1200m	Juwalɛy Sawoʊŋ was born here.
Luwag Lagol 360m	Taaᵏ Lagol ran from a bear; *lagol*, bald.
Cave (*guwɔɔᵏ*)	
Guwɔɔᵏ Taaᵏ Kabɛl	Taaᵏ Kabɛl, a great medium of the Píncoʊŋ River, died here in this cave, before 1950, after hne had retreated here when he was sick. His family came and found his body, so they carried him out of the cave and laid him to rest him nearby.

Person	
River (ʔoʊx)	
ʔOʊx ʔAwaad	A woman, ʔAwaad, went missing around here when all the villagers fled their homes in 1974. They found her after three or four days of searching.
ʔOʊx Kɛdrud	Kɛdrud, is the personal name of a man, ʔAŋah Pandaᵏ, who was born here.
Waterfall (tɛŋkoʊh)	
Tɛŋkoʊh Lagoʊl	Tataaᵏ Lagoʊl, a Menriq, made a cigarette of seven leaves rolled up and put the fire end in his mouth. He then dived into the pool at the bottom, and reappeared in a pool at the top of the waterfall, and his tobacco was still alight. He had special powers and saw six crocodiles in the pool.
River pool (gool)	
Gool ʔAwɛᵏ	The name of a Temiar man, ʔAwɛᵏ ʔAnjaŋ, who bathed at this river pool.
Gool Gohaᵏ	Gohaᵏ Rɛnloʊŋ is a woman who died here.
Gool Hoᵏraᵏ	Jaaᵏ Hoᵏraᵏ was a Temiar woman who fished at the pool.
Gool Lacuh	Taaᵏ Lacuh fell in the river and went around in a whirlpool, and they had to come and help him get out.
Tree (j'huuᵏ)	
Sɛmpaaᵏ Kabɛl	This jungle durian tree belonged to Taaᵏ Kabɛl.
Landing Point (LP)	
B'raboh	The new name given to P'coʊh, after it became a landing point for the Senoi Praaq during the Emergency; English bravo, becomes *b'raboh* in Temiar.

Man-made	
Swidden (l'mog)	
Cɛŋkaar	The house they built here had a floor made of bamboo slats, so they would stay alert, in case of a tiger around at night; *cɛŋkaar*, bamboo strips.
Maníᵏ	A necklace broke and the beads fell on the ground; *maníᵏ*, beads.
P'coʊh	They made the floor with flattened bamboo, and hacked bamboo to make it flat; *coʊh*, which became *p'coʊh*.
Tɛmagaaᵏ	Taaᵏ P'naŋoʊw found a bronze bracelet (made from wire) here; *tɛmagaaᵏ*, bronze.
Mountain (jɛlmoʊl)	
T'naroᵏ 1815m	They made spears here; *taroʊg*, spear, *t'naroʊg*, making of a spear.
Hill (taŋkoʊl)	
Siyoʊy 688m	A man made a nose flute; *siyoʊy*, flute.
Taroʊg 578m	They found wood here for making spears; *taroʊg*, spear.

Man-made	
Gully (luwag)	
Luwag Jawaaj 415m	An iron knife was lost here; *jawaaj*, bush knife.
Luwag S'ləg 212m	A *ləg*, blow-dart quiver, slipped out of a man's loin cloth.
Luwag Tarog 781m	A spear slipped out of the hand and completely disappeared; *tarog*, spear.
Cave (guwɔɔᵏ)	
Guwɔɔᵏ Cíncít	Dream: Tataaᵏ J'raŋkas obtained a ring from a cave soul, while he stayed in the cave over-night; *cíncít*, ring.
Guwɔɔᵏ Garam	While fleeing the bombing, they left a ceramic flask of salt in this cave; *garam*, salt.
River (ʔoʻox)	
ʔOʻox Bɛɛd	Dream: a betel nut pouch fell in the river; *bɛɛd*, pouch.
ʔOʻox Ranjow	ʔAlaŋ Pandaᵏ saw his shadow on the ground, in the evening, and it was long; *ranjow*, tall.
ʔOʻox Sarop	A knife sheath was dropped when they went setting traps and they couldn't find it; *sarop*, sheath.
ʔOʻox Tɛrbaŋ	The new name of the Píncoʻoŋ River, since the aeroplane crash of 1950; *kapal tɛrbaŋ*, aeroplane.
Waterfall (tɛŋkoʻh)	
Tɛŋkoʻh Hoʻoᵏ	A bowl was dropped at the top of this waterfall; *hoʻoᵏ*, bowl.
Tɛŋkoʻh Puran	They dropped a brass lime pot in the waterfall, called a *puran*.
River pool (gool)	
Gool B'laŋaaᵏ	They dropped a wok as they were rafting down the river; *b'laŋaaᵏ*, frying wok.
Gool Pasoʻg	They dropped a plastic bag in the water, that they were using to keep the fish they caught; *pasoʻg*, plastic.
Tree (j'huuᵏ)	
Gərtaᵏ Taaᵏ Jaan	A bridge was laid here by Taaᵏ ʔAmpís (who is also Taaᵏ Jaan) of a *jiyɛɛs* tree trunk; *gərtaᵏ*, bridge.

Crop	
Swidden (l'mog)	
Gawíin	*Kayuh gawíin* is a variety of manioc that was planted here.
Jawaᵏ (2)	They planted *jawaᵏ*, or millet.
Labuᵏ (2)	They planted *labuᵏ*, water gourd, and they had many fruits.
Hill (taŋkoʻl)	
Jawaᵏ 665m	They planted *jawaᵏ*, millet.
K'dɛg 938m	Here they planted manioc and it was bitter; *k'dɛg*, bitter.
Gully (luwag)	
Luwag Padi 303m	They found some stalks of rice growing in the gully; *padi*, rice.

Food	
Swidden *(l'mog)*	
Lacaaŋ	They boiled manioc and it went soft and sticky; *b'lacaŋ*, translucent.
Soh	They camped here to hunt monkeys and often had meat; *soh*, meat.
Mountain *(jɛlmo'l)*	
B'do^k 1302m	They forgot to cut off the stems of the manioc, so it went bad on the way; *c'do^k kayuh*, manioc stems; the name became *b'do^k*.
B'ras 1171m	Taa^k Panda^k spilled rice on the ground up on this mountain, which the Chinese communists had given him; *b'ras*, rice.
Hill *(taŋko'l)*	
Mɛgsag 1058m	They stuffed ferns in bamboo here to cook them; *sax*, to stuff.
Pɛhgooh 673m	They hunted and cooked a monkey in bamboo here; *pɛhgooh*, cooking.
Gully *(luwag)*	
Luwag Nyɛŋ 393m	Here they ate the germ dust of the millet that they had pounded; *nyɛŋ*, to pour into the mouth.
Luwag S'nagad 1017m.	Here they grated *k'waay ʔadɛ^k*, yam, and burned *salɛh* leaf and mixed it in to make it black, and cooked it in bamboo; *sagad*, cooking black yam, *s'nagad*, black yam.
River *(ʔo'o'x)*	
ʔO'o'x Jisaay	They cooked the pith of the *pacɛɛy* palm; *saay*, to shake down into bamboo.
ʔO'o'x Lɛnyo^k	They dropped a manioc root here; *kɛnlo'o'x*, a tuber.
ʔO'o'x Sarɛɛŋ	They had some fish and it tasted bitter; *sarɛɛn*, bitter.
River pool *(gool)*	
Gool Tɛnlaar	They filled bamboo with *so'ic* nuts to soak them in water, to make bait; *tɛnlaar*, soaking.

Custom	
Swidden *(l'mog)*	
C'nɔɔs	They burned *kasay*, a fragrant root, in order to hold off the rain; *c'nɔɔs*, ritual prayer using incense.
S'lipɔɔh	They built a large house where they could hang up the harvested millet and pound the grain. Many people came to help and they danced and sung at night; *pɔɔh*, to dance with bamboo music.
Mountain *(jɛlmo'l)*	
Cɛ^krɛɛ^k 1543m	A child pointed at the mountain, and they said, "*P'raa^k ʔa-cɛ^krɛɛ^k!*" don't point. They were afraid of disturbing the soul of the mountain; *cɛ^krɛɛ^k*, pointing.
Hill *(taŋko'l)*	
Baggo'g 502m	They went to tie traps; *go'g*, to set traps, an avoidance term, to ensure that the trapping is successful.

Custom	
Gully *(luwag)*	
Luwag Candəŋ 393m	The place has many flowers which women use for decorating the hair; *cadùg*, stuff in the hair.
River *(ˀoˊoˊx)*	
ˀOˊoˊx Bajaax	They built a rat-trapping hut, called a *bajaax*.
ˀOˊoˊx Julaaᵏ	*Julaaᵏ* means to do something in secret, to avoid breaking taboo.
ˀOˊoˊx Nɛysoˊoˊy	Dream: they built a shelter here from palm leaves; *nɛysoˊoˊy*, a shelter.
ˀOˊoˊx Sɛmkap	They set rat traps along the river; *kɛm* or *kam*, traps.
Tree *(jˈhuuᵏ)*	
Sɛmpaaᵏ Gˈnalɛɛs	Dream: they were dancing and shaking bunches of fragrant leaves; *gˈnalɛɛs*, shaking of a leaf bunch to procure healing.

GROUP 5: NON-HUMAN FACTORS

Spiritual	
Swidden *(lˈmog)*	
Layan	A *bɛrboˊw* tree, which has a malicious soul, ordered them to make an offering of chicken's blood, or it would cause death in the area; *layan*, to offer.
Soroŋ	A Tataaᵏ halaaᵏ received power; *soroŋ*, to transfer soul-medium power, in a dream.
Hill *(taŋkoˊl)*	
Sˈnəryoˊr 767m	A young man fell into a deep sleep when a *pət'rii*, soul of the mountain, caught his soul away, after he broke a taboo; *sˈnɛryoˊr*, to sleep, unable to wake up.
Gully *(luwag)*	
Luwag Lisaah 1426m	Dream: the *guníg* showed him a *pət'rii* soul and said its name was Lisaah.
Ridge *(gɛrbɔɔᵏ)*	
Gɛrbɔɔᵏ Rantoˊᵏ 388m	Dream: there was an evil *bɛrboˊw* tree, and it ordered them to make an offering or it would eat the people living there; *toᵏ*, to eat, which became *rantoᵏ*.
Cave *(guwɔɔᵏ)*	
Guwɔɔᵏ ˀOoŋ	A woman was led to this cave and held captive some days by the Jaaᵏ ˀAwooy that lived there, whose name was ˀOoŋ. The cave is feared until today.
Waterfall *(tɛŋkoˊh))*	
Tɛŋkoˊh Ləruw	Dream: Taaᵏ Kabɛl dreamed of the soul of the great waterfall here, who was named Taaᵏ Ləruw.
Tree *(jˈhuuᵏ)*	
Badoˊoˊx Taaᵏ Gɛndow	Taaᵏ ˀAmpís found the soul of the tiger which attacked Taaᵏ Gɛndow, in his dream, and he sent it into the *badoˊoˊx* tree to make the Puyan safe again. But it is taboo to cut that tree with a knife.

Catastrophe	
Swidden *(l'mog)*	
C'nantəl	Some children played with a monkey, bathing it in water, and later on a storm came, and the rocks and earth covered them all, and they all died, as they broke the taboo (məsiᵏ); citəl, to crowd, c'nantəl, a crowd.
Lɛŋraaŋ	The early Menriq inhabitants teased a baby macaque monkey. Subsequently, the earth turned over and consumed them all; lɛŋlaaŋ, earthquake.
Hill *(taŋkoʼl)*	
Lɛgliig 956m	A storm came, while it was still midday; lɛgliig, consuming.
Inland pool *(cagool)*	
Cagol Yɛlyool	A group of Jehais spent the night here on their journey from Perak. It rained heavily and began to flood, then a gigantic rock fell on them as they tried to find safer ground; yɛlyool, turning over of the earth.
Bog *(l'baax)*	
Payaᵏ Dɛŋdəx Pɛrsoʼl	Some Menriqs were foraging fruits, and they played with a monkey, laughing at it, giving it a loin cloth. Then disaster struck, with a storm and falling trees, until they were all killed; payaᵏ dɛŋdɛx, storm mud; pɛrsol from tɛrsoʼoj, finished.
Payaᵏ Yɛlyool	This mud pool was formed by the storm and turning over of the land that happened long ago, at Lɛŋraaŋ; payaᵏ, mud, yɛlyool, terrible storm.

Death	
Ridge *(gɛrbɔɔᵏ)*	
C'rɛŋkap	Gɛslas al Mɛndol died here on Soid mountain while walking back from R'kob and had no food. He was found in a crawling position; cɛrkap, to crawl on all fours, c'rɛŋkap, a crawl.
Waterfall *(tɛŋkoʼh)*	
J'rəp L'bíír	Taaᵏ Solah, a Jehai, was attacked and eaten by a tiger on the rock, at the rapid. His blood clotted and formed lumps; j'rəp, rapid; k'baar, to clot, became l'bíír.

Dream	
Swidden *(l'mog)*	
Maŋgəs	Dream: the guníg said, "Gəs, ʔa-maaᵏʷ", come on, let's go back.
Mountain *(jɛlmoʼl)*	
ʔƐnɛŋrɛm 1484m	Dream: a pətt'rii soul, whose name was ʔƐnɛŋrɛm.
ʔƐnoyɛg 1507m	Dream: the guníg pushed aside the bushes at this peak, looking for food; loriyɛg, to wade through the undergrowth.
ʔƐnudɛɛr 1116m	Dream: the guníg was reluctant to go; ʔudɛɛr, to drag one's feet.
K'narɛɛw 1631m	Dream: the guníg called everyone to the mountain-top; garow, to call together, g'narow, calling.

Dream	
Mountain (jɛlmoʼl) – *Continued*	
K'nɛŋrɛɛw 1489m	Taaᵏ ʔAmpís dreamed of a *pət'rii* soul, a princess of the mountain at this peak, who was old and unable to move; *kaŋrəəŋ*, or *k'nɛŋrəəŋ*, stiff.
K'niríŋ 1635m	Dream: they were dancing, and the old man said, "ʔɛ-ʔiríŋ mɛj." From ʔiríŋ, to walk with arms over each other's shoulders.
Lɛᵏŋiᵏ 1585m	Dream: the mountain was named after a *pət'rii* soul which was seen in a dream by Taaᵏ ʔAmpís; the daughter of Taaᵏ Pandaᵏ was also named after this mountain.
Lɛrləər 1394m	Dream: the *guníg* tiger looked down over the valley below; *ləər*, to stretch or view, *lɛrləər*, stretching.
Lírís 1665m	Dream: Taaᵏ ʔAmpís saw a *pət'rii* soul of the mountain and her name was Lírís.
M'naŋgin 1475m	Dream: a *pət'rii* soul, whose name was M'naŋgin.
Pagar 1732m	Dream: the tiger *guníg* showed him that the souls had made a fence around the mountain top; *pagar*, fence.
Paw 1610m	Dream: the *guníg* tiger stamped its paw and made the sound, *paw*.
P'gőy 2109m	Dream: the *guníg* tiger yawned and wanted to sleep; *k'hőy*, yawn, became *p'gőy*.
P'naŋőw 2179m	Dream:Taaᵏ ʔAmpís saw a great tiger on the highest mountain of the region, leaning on its hand; *paŋőw*, to peer, leaning on one's hand.
Ranjőw 1630m	Dream: the *guníg* tiger was standing on the rock, looking tall; *ranjőw*, tall.
S'liwaŋ 1612m	Dream: he dreamed of a dance; *siwaŋ*, to dance, *s'niwaŋ*, ritual dance.
S'numpaag 1785m	Dream: the tiger *guníg* of Taaᵏ ʔAmpís met another *guníg* from downriver, and said to it, "If you come here again I swear you will die!"; *s'numpaag*, an oath.

Masri Pandaᵏ points to P'naŋőw mountain, standing on Lɛmŋőőm.

Dream

Hill *(taŋkoʾl)*

B'latim 742m	Dream: the Tataaᵏ met black-skinned people here in the dream; *b'latɛɛg*, black.
B'nísíg 682m	Dream: the *guníg* spoke quietly, afraid that the jungle souls would hear; *b'nísíg*, a whisper.
Hɛmaay 646m	Dream: Taaᵏ Kabɛl dreamed of a giant caterpillar on this hill; *k'maay*, caterpillar, which became, *hɛmaay*.
Kɛntɨp 871m	Dream: the *guníg* stamped his paw on the ground, angry because he hadn't found anyone to eat; *k'tɨp*, to stamp the foot.
Mɛnjoon 328m	Dream: the *guníg* went along hopping; *pɛnp'joon*, hopping along, which became *mɛnjoon*.
P'naŋʊw 444m	Dream: a tiger was resting on the rock here; *paŋʊw*, to rest on the hand.
Ranal 924m	Dream: Taaᵏ ʾAmpís' *guníg* tiger was contemplating; *ramal*, to think.
Rɛgruwoog 834m	Dream: the *guníg* was singing a Temiar song and prancing along; *rɛgruwoog*, treading like cycling a bike.

Gully *(luwag)*

Luwag ʾƐndəəm 277m	Dream: the *guníg* said in the dream, *"ʾAgoᵏ ʾɛndəəm,"* don't linger.
Luwag Nɛwkơơw 728m	Dream: a tiger called from the forest up there; *nɛwkơơw*, a call.

Boulder *(batuᵏ)*

Batuᵏ Lɛmyíp	Dream: the *gunig* jumped about from one rock to another, until he felt tired; *lɛmyəp*, feeling ill.
Batuᵏ ʾAsal Tajuuᵏ	Dream: this rock outcrop became a giant snake; *tajuuᵏ*, snake; *ʾasal*, ancient.

River *(ʾơơx)*

ʾƠơx B'kəg	Dream: a tiger was shocked at so many people being there; *kəg*, surprised.
ʾƠơx C'rɛɛy	Dream: in the dream a tiger said, *"Jɛᵏ ha-c'rɛɛy ma-yɛiᵏ!"* don't leave me.
ʾƠơx Haŋkal	Dream: the rocks in the river piled up; *haŋkal*, to block the way.
ʾƠơx Hɛnwơơc	Dream: the *gunig* was whistling at the river; *hɛnwơơc*, whistling.
ʾƠơx Kacəŋ	Dream: Pəŋhuluᵏ Bơŋsu dreamed of a tiger walking along in a zig-zag fashion, *dɛŋ-ʾəŋ*, which became *kacəŋ*.
ʾƠơx Pɛndon	Dream: the *gunig*'s tail was curving; *b'dɛŋdơơx*, curved, which became *pɛndon*.
ʾƠơx Puyan	Taaᵏ ʾAmpís met a *guníg* that said to him, "Rantow Puyan," the river given to you by Nyɨᵏ ʾAlɨj the river of *bɛlyan*, power.
ʾƠơx Ragas	Dream: in the dream the *gunig* told them to knock down the perah nuts from the tree; *gas*, to knock off a tree, so the river was named Ragas.

River pool *(gool)*

Gool Jəəx	Dream: there was a crocodile in this river pool whose name was Jəəx.

Tree *(j'huuᵏ)*

Sɛmpaaᵏ Hatơr	Dream: they ran away from a tiger and huddled together in a house; *ʾatơr*, to huddle together.

Army landing point *(LP)*

Ranah	Dream: Taaᵏ ʾAmpis' *gunig* named this place Ranah, but Taaᵏ ʾAmpis added Rɛŋlơŋ to its name as this was the name of a boy born here.

Nyɛbnyaab, red sky at evening, means that evil tigers are prowling.

Temiars of Píɲcoʹoŋ stand in front of Batuᵏ Tajuuᵏ, or Snake Rock, a natural rock formation in the shape of a snake's head (Credit: ʔIdris ʔAsod)

BIBLIOGRAPHY

Baker, A. C. 1933. An account of a journey from the Cameron Highlands to the East Coast Railway and of a visit to the Temiar settlements in the valleys of the Sungai Blatop and S. Ber. *Journal of the Malayan Branch of the Royal Asiatic Society* 11:288-295.

Bedford, K. J. A. 2007. Gombak and its patients: Provision of healthcare to the Orang Asli (indigenous minority) of Peninsular Malaysia. PhD diss., Oxford University.

———. 2009. Gombak Hospital, the Orang Asli hospital. *Indonesia and the Malay World* 37(107): 23–44.

Benjamin, Geoffrey, and C. Chou (eds). 2002. Tribal Communities in the Malay World: Historical, Social and Cultural Perspectives. Leiden/Singapore: International Institute for Asian Studies (IIAS)/Institute of Southeast Asian Studies (ISEAS).

Burkill, I. H. 1935. A dictionary of the economic products of the Malay Peninsula. Kuala Lumpur: Ministry of Agriculture and Cooperatives.

Colchester, Marcus. 1995. Indigenous Peoples' Rights and Sustainable Resource Use in South and Southeast Asia. In R. H. Barnes, A. Gray, and B. Kingsbury (eds); pp. 59-76.

Couillard, Marie-Andreé, 1984. The Malays and the "Sakai": some comments on their social relations in the Malay Peninsula. *Kajian Malaysia: journal of Malaysian studies* 2:81-108.

Dallos, C. 2011. From equality to inequality: Social change among newly sedentary Lanoh hunter-gatherer traders of Peninsular Malaysia. Toronto: University of Toronto Press.

Davison, G. W. H. 1989a. Orang Asli rafts. *Malayan Naturalist* 42(2): 20–21.

———. 1989b. The manufacture and terminology of Temiar bamboo rafts. *Journal of the Malaysian Branch of the Royal Asiatic Society* 62(1): 97–106.

Dentan, Robert K. 1997. The persistence of received truth: How ruling class Malays construct Orang Asli identity. In *Indigenous peoples and the state: Politics, land, and ethnicity in the Malayan Peninsula and Borneo*, Yale Southeast Asia Studies 46, ed. R. L. Winzeler, 98–134. New Haven, CT: Yale University Press.

Dentan, Robert. K., Kirk Endicott, A. G. Gomes and M. B. Hooker 1997. Malaysia and the original people: A case study of the impact of development on indigenous peoples. Boston, MA: Allyn and Bacon.

Dodge, N. 1981. The Malay-aborigine nexus under Malay rule. Bijdragen Tot de Taal-, Land- en Volkenkunde 137(1): 1–16.

Dove, M. R. 2006. Indigenous People and Environmental Politics. *Annual Reviews in Anthropology*, 35: 191–208.

Dunn, Frederick L. 1975. Rain-forest collectors and traders: a study of resource utilization in modern and ancient Malaya. Kuala Lumpur: Malaysian branch of the Royal Asiatic Society.

Endicott, Kirk. 1974. Batek Negrito Economy and Social Organization. Ph.D. dissertation, Harvard University.

———. 1979. The impact of economic modernisation on the Orang Asli (Aborigines) of northern Peninsular Malaysia. In *Issues in Malaysian Development*, J. C. Jackson and M. Rudner (eds). Singapore: Heinemann. Pp. 167-204.

———. 1983. The Effects of Slave Raiding on the Aborigines of the Malay Peninsula. In *Slavery, Bondage, and Dependency in Southeast Asia*, edited by A. Reid and J. Brewster. Brisbane: Queensland University Press, pp. 216-245.

Gray, Andrew. 1995. The indigenous movement in Asia. In R. H. Barnes, Andrew Gray & Benedict Kingsbury (eds), Indigenous Peoples of Asia, Ann Arbor, MI: Association for Asian Studies, pp. 35– 58.

Hill, R.D. 1977. Rice in Malaya: a study in historical geography. Kuala Lumpur: Oxford University Press.

Holman, Dennis, 1958. Noone of the Ulu. London: Heinemann.

Idris, Rusaslina. 2008. The politics of inclusion: Law, history and indigenous rights in Malaysia. PhD diss., Harvard University.

_____. 2010. From Wards to Citizens: Indigenous Rights and Citizenship in Malaysia, *PoLAR: Political and Legal Anthropology Review,* 33(1): 89–108.

Lim, H. F. 1997. Orang Asli, forest and development. *Malayan Forest Records no. 43.* Kuala Lumpur: Forest Research Institute of Malaysia.

Lim, T. G. and A. G. Gomes. eds. 1990. Tribal peoples and development in Southeast Asia. Kuala Lumpur: Department of Anthropology and Sociology, University of Malaya.

Lye, Tuck-Po. 2004. Changing pathways: Forest degradation and the Batek of Pahang, Malaysia. Lanham, MD: Lexington Books.

———. 2005. The road to equality? Landscape transformation and the Batek of Pahang, Malaysia. In *Property and equality: Encapsulation, commercialisation, discrimination,* vol. 2, eds. T. Widlok and W. G. Tadesse, 90–103. Oxford: Berghahn.

Nah, A. M. 2006. (Re)Mapping Indigenous "Race"/Place in Postcolonial Peninsular Malaysia, *Geografiska Annaler,* 88B: 285–297.

Nicholas, Colin. 1992. Orang Asli swiddeners: Scapegoats for forest destruction. Kuala Lumpur: Center for Orang Asli Concerns.

———. 2000. The Orang Asli and the contest for resources: Indigenous politics, development and identity in Peninsular Malaysia. Copenhagen: International Work Group for Indigenous Affairs and Subang Jaya, Malaysia: Center for Orang Asli Concerns.

———. 2003. The Orang Asli: First on the land, last in the plan. *Kajian Malaysia* 21(1 & 2): 315–329.

Nicholas, C., A. Williams-Hunt and Tiah, S. 1989. Orang Asli in the news: The Emergency years, 1950–1958. Petaling Jaya, Malaysia: Center for Orang Asli Concerns.

Nobuta, T. 2009. Living on the periphery: Development and Islamization of the Orang Asli. Subang Jaya, Malaysia: Center for Orang Asli Concerns.

Short, A. 2000. In pursuit of mountain rats: The Communist insurrection in Malaya. Singapore: Cultured Lotus Pte. Ltd.

Siddique, S., and L. Suryadinata 1981/82 Bumiputera and Pribumi. Economic Nationalism (Indigenism) in Malaysia and Indonesia. *Pacific Affairs* 54/4: 662-687.

Subramaniam, Y. 2013. Affirmative Action and the Legal Recognition of Customary Land Rights in Peninsular Malaysia: The Orang Asli Experience. *Australian Indigenous Law Review,* 17(1): 103–122.

ABOUT THE AUTHOR

David P. Quinton, born in England, in 1977, was introduced to the Malay communities of Kelantan in Malaysia when he was only 19 years old. Ten years later, he made his first acquaintance with the Temiar people, at Kuala Betis, on the Nenggiri River. Later, in 2010, he reached the hinterland Temiars of Pos Simpor and Pos Gob. His fascination with their way of life and the knowledge of the environment they held, being so isolated from the outside world, not to mention their gentleness and deep beliefs, led David to begin a journey of investigation into their origins. This is described in the Preface of Vol.1, about his trekking in the forest, and interviewing the old folks among them. In 2016, David married a Temiar and settled down at the Pinchong River, near Pos Gob. They now have two young children, who are growing up in the Temiar way, surrounded by forest and waterfalls.

David's wife, Ella, has been an invaluable source of information regarding Temiar culture, and her guidance has helped to steer the book writing on many occasions. Her father, Samsudin B'ked, and her grandparents, ˀAbus Sisam and ˀAsuh ˀAti, and great uncle, ˀAlɨj Sisam, who are all pictured or mentioned in the book, have provided not only a wealth of knowledge that would have been impossible to discover otherwise, but they have also offered unceasing support to David while he has been living among them. David has planted over 50 fruit trees, from durians to coconuts, and each year he also plants manioc and peanuts. But with elephants on the rampage at night pulling up the manioc and pushing over banana trees, David has experienced first hand the difficulties that now face the Temiars in their endeavor to find food for their families.

The author welcomes feedback on his work and can be contacted by the email address in the front of the book. He is currently working on a grammar of Temiar and a dictionary with some 4000 entries and hopes to publish these in the near future. He also posts some of his latest work on Figshare, including videos of the Temiars and audio recordings of traditional dance music and folktale telling.

Link to his Figshare profile: https://figshare.com/authors/David_P_Quinton/12966872

Above: The author holds an interview with the elders of Píɲcoʼoŋ village. From left to right: the late ʔAhíŋ Bərlɛɛy, ʔAlʉj Sisam, Samsudin Bʼkəd and ʔAbus Sisam.
Below: ʔElla Samsudin sits with her mother ʔAndaᵏ ʔAbus, and her grandmother, ʔAsuh ʔAti.

Ingram Content Group UK Ltd.
Milton Keynes UK
UKHW050640270723
425851UK00004B/11